P9-AFX-798

child magazine's book of

CHILDREN'S
PARTIES

child magazine's book of

CHILDREN'S
PARTIES

ANGELA WILKES

A DORLING KINDERSLEY BOOK

Editors
Caroline Greene • Annelise Evans

Designers
Emma Boys • Tracey Clarke

Art Editor
Karen Ward

US Editor
Laaren Brown

Managing Editors
Jemima Dunne • Maureen Rissik

Managing Art Editor
Philip Gilderdale

DTP Designer
Karen Ruane

Production
Maryann Rogers

Photography
Susanna Price
Tim Ridley
Clive Streeter

First American edition, 1996
2 4 6 8 10 9 7 5 3 1
Published in the United States by DK Publishing, Inc.
95 Madison Avenue, New York, NY 10016

Copyright © 1996 Dorling Kindersley Limited, London
Text copyright © 1996 Angela Wilkes

All rights reserved under International and Pan-American Copyright
Conventions. No part of this publication may be reproduced, stored in a
retrieval system, or transmitted in any form or by any means, electronic,
mechanical, photocopying, recording, or otherwise, without the prior
written permission of the copyright owner. Published in Great Britain
by Dorling Kindersley Limited.
Distributed by Houghton Mifflin Co., Boston.

Library of Congress Cataloging-in-Publication Data
Child magazine's book of children's parties. -- 1st American ed.
    p.   cm.
    Includes index.
    ISBN 1-56458-853-X
    1. Children's parties. I. Child magazine.
GV1205.C48   1996
793.2'1--dc20   95-44328
                                              CIP

"**child**" is a registered trademark of Gruner & Jahr USA Publishing.

Reproduced in Hong Kong by Bright Arts
Printed and bound in Singapore by Star Standard Industries

Publisher's note
Throughout this book, the pronouns "he" and "she" refer to both sexes,
except where a topic applies specifically to a boy or girl. The term
"parents" refers to parents, a parent, or a guardian.

FOREWORD

Whenever we publish a birthday party article in **child** magazine, our readers thank us profusely for giving them ideas to help top last year's bash. So it's no wonder we're eager to introduce an entire book packed with plans for party food, games, favors, cakes, and decorations. Organized in a helpful age-by-age format, this book will inspire you to create a party perfectly suited to your child's taste, temperament, and stage of development. We've kept in mind parental concerns, too, like budget, space, and easy recipes. We know parties, but only you know your child, so mix and match from the hundreds of ideas we've assembled here, and have yourselves the most excellent celebration ever!

Pamela Abrams
Editor-in-Chief, **child** magazine

CONTENTS

PARTY PLANNING
*All you need to know to ensure
a successful party*

DECORATIONS & THEMES
*Turn a party into an adventure with
these inspiring and practical ideas*

PARTY GAMES
*Indoor and outdoor games and
activities for all age groups*

PARTY FOOD
*Easy-to-make recipes for delicious
party food and drinks*

FIRST AID
*Basic guidelines on first aid
for minor accidents 72*

PARTY PLANNING

Careful preparation will make a party a happy occasion for the guests, and a low-stress experience for you.

Party Planning Tips

◊ Keep the duration of the party short and the number of guests small.

◊ Mail invitations (pages 28–29) in plenty of time. Supervise your child handing them out at school, or you may create hurt feelings.

◊ Plan everything well ahead of the party: the location, the guests, the decorations, menu, games, activities, props, and treats. For reference, keep lists of everything you will need.

◊ Don't be too ambitious. Keep the party simple, with one special activity or feature. Most small children have very short attention spans.

◊ Involve the birthday child as much as possible in the preparations, but don't force a reluctant child.

◊ For a party at home, decide which areas of the house or yard will be out of bounds to small guests.

◊ For an outing, keep the party small and take along several helpers. An outing can be as simple as a picnic in the park, or a football game with cake back at home. It could be a trip to a zoo, pool, or the movies.

◊ If you use a party place, book well in advance. Check if supervision is provided and confirm the reservation in writing. Call a few days before the party to check that all is in order.

◊ Write out a party plan, with the games in order of play. Remember, children may only spend 20–30 minutes eating the party meal.

◊ Arrange to have at least one adult helper. For a toddler's party, you may need several helpers.

◊ To prevent conflict, keep any gifts for the birthday child to open after the guests have left – although many guests consider the opening a party highlight.

◊ Arrange all your props, goodie bags, and music tapes in boxes beforehand and tell your helper where they are.

◊ Shut away pets, such as dogs, that may frighten or hurt young children.

◊ Keep a list of the guests' home telephone numbers to hand, in case of upsets or emergencies.

◊ Tell guests where to leave their coats and where the bathroom is.

PLANNING A PARTY
FOR A
1- OR 2-YEAR-OLD

Very young children do not understand what a party is, so a first or second birthday party will be a special celebration for family and friends at which the child simply enjoys the fun.

Two-year-old
He is still vague about birthdays.

Cheesy shapes
(page 57)

Accordion-fold invitation
Toddlers find these simple shapes (page 28) fascinating to play with.

Stuffed toys
These make ideal playthings or going-home gifts.

Guests
For a child's first birthday party, you may want to ask a few relatives, but remember that a baby can be overwhelmed by a large group. Have a joint party with two or three friends who have babies the same age. For two-year-olds, invite four or five children with parents. Plan a lunch or afternoon party of 1–1½ hours.

Invitations
Choose bold colors and strong shapes, like a favorite animal, for invitations. Cutouts (page 28) are fun: thread a ribbon through the top of each one so that guests can hang them up in their bedrooms.

Decorations
Keep these simple: hang a few bright streamers out of reach. Don't use balloons; they may frighten young children and can be a choking hazard.

One-year-old
Supply lots of cushions and bright, chunky toys.

The table is the focus of the party, so use a disposable tablecloth, napkins, and plates with a cheerful party design, and include settings for the parents. For two-year-olds, you could set out a child-sized table and small chairs. Ask the parents to bring each child's drinking bottle or sippy cup.

Menu
Babies and toddlers like to pick at party finger foods and usually drink a large amount, so aim to provide a few tempting goodies (pages 54–69), such as little sandwiches, finger food like cucumber or carrot sticks that have been softened by blanching, pastry shapes, picture cookies, tiny cupcakes, small portions of ice cream, birthday cake, and plenty of milk and diluted fruit juice.

Adult guests may eat some of the finger food with the children, but provide extra refreshments for adult tastes. Try open sandwiches, canapés, sparkling fruit punch, and fruit salad.

Toys
One-year-olds don't yet play together, but often play alongside one another with separate toys. Put cushions on the floor and lay out board books, stuffed toys, balls, rattles, and soft building blocks. Add bigger toys with wheels (cars, trucks, trains) for toddlers. For a toddler's summer party, set out a low activity center or small slide in the yard, and put out tricycles and pedal cars for the children to play with.

Star cake
Use colorful icing in a simple pattern (page 65).

Finger food
Serve crunchy tidbits for the children and add savory dips for the parents (page 54).

Playtime

There is no need to organize games for this age group, because they are happy just to play with toys. They do enjoy a little musical entertainment, however. Have a cassette player ready with nursery-rhyme tapes, so that children can dance if they want to. With two-year-olds, try activities such as Here We Go Round the Mulberry Bush (page 38) or Musical Bumps (page 42). Make a few basic instruments from household objects (page 43) and have a musical parade through the house or yard.

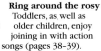

Ring around the rosy
Toddlers, as well as older children, enjoy joining in with action songs (pages 38–39).

Going-home treats

For each child, wrap a small gift in a round bag of colored tissue paper or wrapping paper (page 35). Choose small toys that are safety-approved for children under three years old.

You could give one-year-olds different board books or bath books, bath toys, squeaky toys, or party hats. Two-year-olds like small packs of chunky wax crayons, paint-with-water books, colorful toy animals, and novelty bath sponges.

Two-year-old
At this age, a party is a novelty and a time to have fun.

PARTY PLAN

Keep the party simple and be prepared to adapt if children are grumpy or need distracting.

◊ Children arrive and play with toys.

◊ Serve drinks to parents.

◊ Help birthday child open the presents (optional).

◊ Party meal. Take photographs or shoot a video.

◊ Children play with books and toys, or in the yard.

◊ Musical entertainment.

◊ Going-home time and treats.

PARTY TIPS

◊ "Babyproof" the party rooms. Make sure breakable objects are out of reach and that there are no sharp corners on which to bump heads.

◊ Put up a stair gate. Install outlet covers in all sockets and tie up curtain cords.

◊ To avoid tears, put away your child's favorite toys.

◊ Do not serve any hard candies, nuts, popcorn, hot dogs, or small fruits to the children; they could choke.

◊ Ask a friend to serve the adults during the meal.

◊ Don't play games for too long; babies and toddlers have very short attention spans and can become tired easily.

◊ Play Sleeping Lions (page 40) to calm the children down just before they go home.

PLANNING A PARTY
— FOR A —
3-YEAR-OLD

Balloons
Hang balloons
up out of reach.

*By the time children are three, they are beginning to understand
what parties are all about. The key elements of the party for a birthday
child are "my friends, presents, and a cake with candles."*

Crepe streamers
Use bold colors
(page 30).

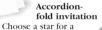

**Accordion-
fold invitation**
Choose a star for a
shape theme (page 28).

Hot potato
Music and a ball
combine in a
great game
(page 43).

Novelty straw
Cut out and decorate a
2in (5cm) paper "face"
and slide it onto a straw.

Guests

Your child may now have special
friends at a play group or nursery
school. Invite no more children than
will fit around your table; about six is
ideal. Plan a lunch or afternoon party
of 1½–2 hours. Most three-year-olds
are not yet independent enough to
stay without their parents.

Invitations

Try making accordion-fold or
cutout invitations (page 28), using
a simple color or shape theme
(page 20) – for example, make a
spotted bear or a pink elephant.
Your child can help you choose
which shapes to make and can
even help you decorate them.

Decorations

Decorate the party room with
simple streamers and balloons out
of reach of the children. You
could introduce an animal theme,
or colors and shapes, for this age
group (pages 20–23). Focus your
efforts on the party table and
make it as colorful as possible.
Have a decorative disposable
tablecloth, plates, and cups.
Write the guests' names on
party hats (pages 32–33), put
one on each plate, and make a
game of finding the right seat.

Menu

Be inventive and cut small treats
into familiar animal shapes or
decorate with colorful patterns.

Try these party dishes and drinks
(pages 54–70): tiny open sandwiches,
cheesy wands and hearts, tomato
treats, picture cookies, iced cupcakes,
ice cream, choco-milk, and fruit
juices diluted with water.

Make a special cake that looks like
your child's favorite animal or toy
(pages 62–69). Remember to provide
enough food and drink for the
children's parents (page 8).

Toys

Provide plenty of toys for this age
group, as there are always some
children who are reluctant or too shy
to join in games. Three-year-olds will
spend much of a party in free play.
Put out dolls and stuffed toys, toy
cars and trains, picture books, simple
jigsaws, a dress-up box, and a

Feely bag
Three-year-olds can cope with
easy guessing games (page 44).

⚠ CAUTION!
Balloons can be a
choking hazard.

Cupcakes
Ice these and decorate
with patterns or faces (page 59).

PARTY PLAN

◊ Children arrive and play.

◊ Birthday child opens gifts
(optional).

◊ Serve drinks to parents.

◊ Play Follow the Leader.

◊ Action songs or hand rhymes.

◊ Party meal. Take photographs
or shoot a video.

◊ Play two or three games.

◊ Children's free play.

◊ Party bags
and going-
home
time.

"messy" corner with finger paints and
nontoxic modeling clay – provide
smocks to protect the children's
clothes. If the weather permits, put
a low activity center, sandbox, or
wading pool in the yard. Always
supervise children closely,
especially around water.

Games

Choose about four short and easy
games (pages 38–49). Three-year-olds
love almost any musical or copying
game. Avoid competitive games that
can lead to tears among the losers.
If you want to give treats, keep them
small and present one to every child
as a reward for their efforts. Try the
following games: any action songs
or hand rhymes, Sleeping Lions,
Mr. Bear's Footsteps, Pass the Bundle,
Musical Bumps, Match the Balloon,
Follow the Leader, Roll a Ball, and
Making Bubbles.

Going-home treats

Make a colorful fabric or paper party
bag (page 35) for each child. Fill
each bag with four or five small gifts,
such as stickers, plastic farm animals,
crayons, wriggly snakes, blowers, toy
cars, small picture books, or soft
balls. Check that the items are all safe
for three-year-old children.

Three-year-old
A birthday party
can be very
exciting for
children of
this age.

PARTY TIPS

◊ Move any breakable items or
favorite toys to a room that is
out of bounds.

◊ Enlist one or two of the
guest parents as helpers
beforehand; give them a copy
of the party plan.

◊ Ask your helpers to play
with any shy guests while you
supervise the games.

◊ Be flexible. Three-year-olds
can be temperamental and may
not want to join in organized
games at all. If so, encourage
them to play with the toys.

◊ If the children become too
boisterous, sit them down for
some hand rhymes or a really
quiet game, such as Sleeping
Lions, or read them a story.

◊ If one child is disruptive,
separate him from the others
and give him a little job to do.

PLANNING A PARTY
FOR A
4-YEAR-OLD

Four-year-olds are very enthusiastic about parties. Party themes and games come into their own and the birthday child will enjoy helping you plan the festivities.

Mystery bundle
This guessing game (page 44) is great fun.

Plate mask
Make animal masks like this bear (page 32).

Dress-up invitation
A guest can cut out this harlequin mask to wear (page 29).

Pin the tail on the donkey
Children always like traditional games (page 41).

Princess hat
Make this (page 33) for a fairy-tale or kings and queens theme party.

Guests

Aim to invite six to ten guests to a party for this age group. Ask your child which friends he wants to invite to the party and only ask relatives with whom the child is comfortable. You can ask parents to leave the children at the party and pick them up about two hours later, although there may be many children who still prefer their parents to stay with them (more helpers for you!). Make sure that you have at least one adult to help you with hosting the party.

Invitations

Children might be able to draw simple pictures by now, so why not use one of your child's drawings as a basis for high-tech invitations? You could make photocopies or computer printouts (page 29) and ask the child to color them in. Alternatively, make cutout invitations (page 28) and let the child decorate them. For a theme, send dress-up invitations (page 28).

Decorations

Four-year-olds may have very definite ideas about the decorations or party theme, so enlist their help. Dinosaurs and monsters are popular; you could adapt the ideas on animal themes (page 23) for such a theme. Cut out large shapes, ask your child to decorate them, and hang them on the walls. Make animal streamers (page 30) or a mobile (page 31) to hang above the table. Match the table decorations to the theme and give the guests paper streamers to throw.

Menu

Plan a varied menu of sweet and savory food (pages 54–71) and tie it in to a theme. Keep the portions small. Try open sandwiches, a porcupine or dinosaur made from a chunky dip and vegetable sticks, picture pizzas, chips, iced cupcakes, fruit salads, and a dinosaur cake (a dragon cake decorated with spots instead of scales), with ruby fruit punch, or real strawberry shakes.

Toys

Arrange a quiet corner with books and jigsaw puzzles for shy guests who prefer not to join in the games.

I'm a little teapot
Four-year-olds still enjoy action songs (page 39).

Dragon cake
Children love dragons and monsters, so make a cake to suit their tastes (page 64).

Picture pizzas
Make these exciting with toppings and garnishes (page 57).

Warm-up activities

Four-year-olds enjoy making things, so prepare some craft activities to break the ice when the children arrive (page 47). Make masks and hats (pages 32–33) and provide felt pens and sticker shapes so that the children can decorate them. Draw a bold mural on art-roll paper for the guests to color in together.

Games

At this age, children are enthusiastic about games. Explain the rules slowly and be prepared to help. Plan up to eight games (pages 38–50) to last five minutes each. Avoid competitive games; play ones that are just fun or where everyone wins a treat. Adapt games to a theme by renaming them and using suitable props. Choose from Feed the Lion, Monkey's Tail, Stop!, Guess the Sound, Feely Bag, Balloon Race, Who Has the Key?, Bowling, Freeze Tag, Duck, Duck, Goose, and the Parachute Game.

Prizes and treats

Put tiny wrapped treats (blowers, pencils, novelty erasers, bubbles, soap shapes) in a basket and ask the birthday child to hand them out as prizes. For going home, write the guests' names on small wrapped presents (sticker books, small plastic toys, etc.), hide them, and have a treasure hunt as the last game.

Four-year-old
Games are played with energy and enthusiasm at this age.

PARTY PLAN

◇ Children arrive.

◇ Birthday child opens the presents (optional).

◇ Children decorate party hats, masks, or mural, or do other craft activities.

◇ Play two or three games.

◇ Party meal. Take photographs or shoot a video.

◇ Play four or five more games.

◇ Play Hunt the Present for going-home presents.

◇ Going-home time.

PARTY TIPS

◇ Prepare a few more games than you think you will need, just in case the children race through them.

◇ Give your helpers a list of the games. Tell them where the props are and how to work the cassette player.

◇ Make sure the birthday child gets a treat while he is handing out prizes.

◇ If the children become too rowdy, ask them to sit down and put their hands on their heads. Wait until they are all silent, then play a copying game, such as Simon Says. When they have quieted down, continue with your party plan.

◇ Restrict the treasure hunt to one room to protect your furniture, knickknacks and other breakables.

PLANNING A PARTY
— FOR A —
5-YEAR-OLD

A five-year-old child is more grown-up in many ways than a four-year-old. This allows you far more scope in planning a party.

Party polaroids
These make an amusing going-home gift.

Picture roll
Make bread rolls fun for hungry party-goers (page 55).

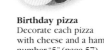

Birthday pizza
Decorate each pizza with cheese and a ham number "5" (page 57).

Red potion
Mix a colorful cocktail of fruit juices (page 70).

Ice-cream sundae
This strawberry sundae is one of many popular varieties (page 60).

Fairy-tale cottage cake (page 66)

Guests

Your child may want to invite the whole class to the party. Unless you are going to a party place and have lots of helpers, restrict the number of guests to no more than ten. Plan a party of 2–2½ hours. Five-year-olds soon wear themselves out and become cranky if expected to behave sociably for longer.

Invitations

Make invitations that tie in with the party theme (pages 28–29) and ask your child to help you make them.

Decorations

With this age group, try more ambitious themes: pirates, wizards and witches, and fairy tales are popular. Decorate the game room, as well as the party table. Your child could help with making streamers (pages 30–31). Hang up balloons decorated with funny faces. If you prepare the materials in advance, the guests can finish off the decorations as a warm-up activity.

Special attractions

Children of this age are beginning to develop their own interests, so you may want to plan something special. Ask the children to wear costumes, or hire an entertainer, or put on a simple magic show. An energetic child would enjoy an outdoor party with races and ball games, or a visit to the local swimming pool or gym, with a party meal at home afterward.

Costume parties

Many five-year-olds really relish a costume party. Ask them to come to the party in a costume, or provide a box of appropriate clothing for them to put on when they arrive. A hat, cloak, or scarf, and a suitable prop will usually do the trick. If any child is reluctant to dress up, tempt him or her with a small item, such as a stick-on mustache or a headband (page 32). If you know someone who is good at face painting, ask the artist to come and paint the children's faces.

Menu

Many children at this age are hungry after games, but are still picky eaters. The spread should be varied and colorful (pages 54–71). Make picture rolls, mini quiches, picture pizzas, tomato treats, party pretzels, chocolate crispies, fruit kebabs, ice-cream sundaes, birthday cake, and real lemonade or sunset punch.

Hide the cake until the party so that it is a surprise for the birthday child as well as for everyone else.

Race-track game (page 45)

Wizard's costume
Decorate a conical hat (page 33) and a cape with silver moons and stars.

Plate mask
This lion face is easy to make (page 32).

Games

Games will be the high point of the party. Plan 10–12, with a variety of quiet and energetic games, team games, and memory games or brainteasers (pages 40–50). Make it easier for yourself by choosing a few games that don't need props. No game should last longer than 7–10 minutes, or boredom may set in. Try Feed the Lion, Pass the Bundle, Hot Potato, Stop!, Feely Bag, Guess What?, Memory Game, Balloon Race, Treasure Hunt, Freeze Tag, Duck, Duck, Goose, Parachute Game, or Dress-Up Race.

Prizes and treats

For a costume party, wrap up face paints, false noses, or plastic jewelry. Put small toys linked to the theme, such as erasers, pencils, and stickers, in a prize chest (page 35) for guests to take a treat before they go home. Give each guest a polaroid of him- or herself taken at the party, and a slice of cake in a napkin.

Five-year-old
She will look forward to a party for weeks in advance.

PARTY PLAN

◊ Children arrive. Birthday child opens presents (optional).

◊ Children dress up or have their faces painted. Take polaroid photographs.

◊ Children finish decorations.

◊ Play three or four games.

◊ Party meal. Take the photos or shoot a video.

◊ Magic show, entertainer, or other special activity, if any.

◊ Play four or six more games.

◊ Prize chest.

◊ Going-home time.

PARTY TIPS

◊ Put out all the props for the first activity in advance.

◊ Clear as much furniture as you can from the game room.

◊ Be vigilant with the games. Team games are still difficult at this age. You may have to act as a tactful referee and intercede if the children's tempers start to fray.

◊ Keep the momentum of the party going and avoid slow spots between the games, activities, and the party meal.

◊ Keep an eye on bossy or dominant guests and don't allow them to take over the games. If they persist, suggest that they help you out with refereeing the games.

◊ Remember to let the birthday child start off as many games as possible.

15

Planning a Party
for
Mixed Ages

If the children are not all of the same age, plan the party to suit the age of the majority, but make concessions for the younger or older children.

Party medal
A child will be proud to wear this (page 35).

Cupcake
This cat face (page 59) has great appeal.

Party bag
Give a similar bag (page 35) to each child, but vary the contents according to age.

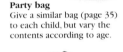

Mixed ages
Most young children play together happily, but need a little tactful supervision!

Party meal
Unless you have a very large table, it is a good idea to have a separate, smaller table and chairs for younger children at a party. That way they are less likely to be pushed or jostled by the bigger children and you can serve them a few special tidbits to suit their smaller appetites. Give them boxes of juice with straws, instead of cups or glasses.

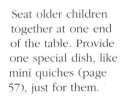

Seat older children together at one end of the table. Provide one special dish, like mini quiches (page 57), just for them.

Games
Many of the games on pages 38–50 are suitable for most young children, as long as you help the smaller ones. Very young children cannot cope with memory games or brainteasers, so provide a quiet toy corner for them to play in while the older guests are playing the more demanding games. Ask your helpers to look after the younger guests if you are too busy.

Older children can easily become bored at a party for toddlers, but they often like helping. Ask them to help you with the cassette player or with refereeing and judging any games. Another option is to set up an activities corner where they can make things like hats (page 47).

Prizes and treats
Make two prize chests (page 35), each with treats suitable for one age group. For going home, treat all the children the same by giving individually tagged party bags or baskets (pages 34–35) and tailoring the contents to the guest's age.

Wibbly wobbly game
Older children enjoy this game (page 48) as much as the younger ones.

TROUBLESHOOTING

Candies
Don't give out
too many.

*Even the best-planned party can have minor calamities! Young
children are emotional and can become overexcited or tearful.
Here are suggestions on dealing with common situations.*

**Summer ice
pop** (page 60)

Your child's role

A birthday child can easily build
false expectations of what is going
to happen at the party. He or she
may expect to win every game or
to tell everyone what to do. Run
through your party plan with your
child beforehand and make him feel
special by allowing him to start as
many games as possible.

Guest refuses to stay

Reassure the retiring child that the
parent can stay. Encourage the child
by describing the special activities
or treats that lie in store and drop
names of friends who will be there.

A brother or sister is upset

Brothers and sisters are often
jealous of a birthday child. Explain
to them that they will be the focus
of attention on *their* birthday, when
it will be their turn to have the
party and all the presents. You
could give them their own special
party task, such as helping you with
the props for games, or passing
around food at the table.

Child does not join in

Try gentle encouragement, but don't
persist. Suggest that the child play
with toys or look at books. If the
child is totally uncooperative, leave
him or her alone, but check in from
time to time.

Overexcited and rowdy guests

Play a quiet game such as Sleeping
Lions (page 40), which requires no
extra props, or read the children
a story. Brainteasers such as the
Memory Game (page 45) demand

some quiet concentration. With all
parties for older children, it is a
good idea to make some rooms in
your home out of bounds and to
discourage running around upstairs.

Child not winning prizes

The best way to avoid this is not
to have competitive games at all.
Adapt the rules of games (pages
38–50) wherever possible so that
there is no one overall winner, but
several. Reward as many guests as
possible with praise, candies, or
small prizes. Alternatively, try to

After the party
Save one gift to unwrap
after the guests have gone.

manipulate the games to ensure that
each child wins in turn; this is easy
to do with musical games, where
you decide when to stop the music.

Unexpected guests

An extra guest or two sometimes
turns up at a party; usually the child
is a guest's sibling. To avoid tears
and tantrums, make sure that you
have extra party plates and cups
available, and prepare a few
additional treats and goodie bags
(page 35) to keep in reserve.

Rain at an outdoor party

When planning an outdoor party,
always have a rainy-day plan up
your sleeve. Have an indoor picnic
by clearing a space and spreading
a cloth on the floor. Some outdoor
games (pages 48–50) can be adapted
for play inside, but make sure you
prepare some indoor games as a
contingency measure.

Minor accidents

If a child is hurt during the rough-
and-tumble of the party, apply first
aid as described on pages 72–78.
Remove the debris of any breakages
at once to avoid injury.

Winding down

When all the guests have left, the
birthday child may feel a bit forlorn.
Instead of rushing to clean up, sit
down with your child and look at
the presents, read one of the
birthday books, or try out one of the
new games together. If you have an
only child, ask one best friend to
stay and play for a little while. Then
it is bath, story, and bedtime.

DECORATIONS & THEMES

Decorations, whether on the table or all over the house, immediately create a festive atmosphere. If you have a theme, your guests can join in the fun by dressing up.

Party Themes
Make the party a special experience by adapting the invitations, decorations, games, treats, and food to one theme.

Making Invitations
Announce your party with these novel, hand-crafted invitations to get your guests in a party mood.

Making Decorations
These ideas for colorful streamers, paper chains, pom-poms, balloons, and mobiles can be adapted to fit any party theme.

Making Masks & Hats
Lots of great hats and masks can all be adapted from a few basic designs for a costume party or a craft activity.

Treats & Prizes
Use these suggestions for choosing, wrapping, and presenting party prizes and going-home treats.

Decorations & Themes Tips

◊ Decide well in advance whether you will have a party theme or a special feature for the party, so that you can plan accordingly.

◊ Party themes are lots of fun for children of three years and older, but don't feel obliged to have one. The party can be great without one.

◊ If your child is going through a craze for a particular idea, such as pirates, plan a theme around it.

◊ Choose envelopes before making your invitations, and cut out the invitations to fit the envelopes.

◊ On each invitation, give the date and place of the party, the start and end times, and a phone number for the RSVP. Say if there will be a theme or costumes.

◊ Put a footnote on the invitations asking the parents to notify you if any child has an allergy or condition such as asthma.

◊ If short of time, photocopy the invitation and ask your child to help you color them in.

◊ If you don't have much time or money, concentrate on decorating the table and hang up lots of streamers, or just make one huge decoration, such as a mobile.

◊ Before making the decorations, stock up with useful materials, such as posterboard and foil, crepe and tissue paper, glue, tape, gummed shapes, and glitter.

◊ Set aside an afternoon with your children for gluing and pasting.

◊ Make a shopping list for the prizes and treats. Buying small items such as erasers or party blowers in packs is less costly.

◊ To make sure that you have enough items, sort the prizes into order of play and buy or make party bags and fill them well in advance.

◊ Prepare a surplus of prizes and going-home treats and keep them on hand for unexpected guests.

◊ Make the table look festive with a colorful tablecloth and paper party plates, cups, name cards, and novelty drinking straws. These are available at supermarkets or party stores.

Colors & Shapes

Understanding color and pattern is an important part of early learning, so this theme is ideal for the younger age group.

Party mobile
Make one (page 31) with colored streamers.

Colored paper
Follow a color theme with bright candy wrappers and crepe streamers (page 30).

Accordion-fold invitation
Choose a simple shape in the party colors (page 28).

Creating the theme
This is the simplest and the most flexible of themes. Choose any color or pattern, or a combination, and make all the decorations in the same hues and shapes. Start with your child's favorite color, or the child's initial – for instance, "P" is for Pam and purple. Shapes such as polka dots, hearts, or stripes are good bases for a theme. Your child could help you by coloring in the invitations. Ask the guests to wear clothes in the theme patterns or colors, and help them to decorate colored headbands (pages 32 & 47) at the party.

Games, prizes, and food
Wrap bundles for games in the party color or pattern, and give prizes such as soap shapes or finger paints. Play color-matching games or change game titles to fit, such as Feed the Polka-Dot Dog (page 40). A few colors, like blue, are not ideal for food, but with inventive icing and garnishes, most patterns and combinations of colors are possible.

Streamer hat
Make costumes with clothes in the party colors and top them off with a hat like this (page 32).

Prizes and treats
Wrap going-home treats in the party colors (page 35).

Party table
Dress up the table with a paper tablecloth, cups, plates, and party straws in bold colors.

Cutout invitation
Make this (page 28) in the number shape of the child's age.

RAINBOWS

For this party, choose a combination of several colors and stripes. If the weather is good, you could have a rainbow party outdoors.

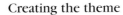

Cupcakes
Different-colored toppings create a rainbow on a plate.

Multicolored T-shirt
Children's clothes in rainbow stripes are easy to find.

Creating the theme

Base the colors of the party on the seven colors of the rainbow (red, orange, yellow, green, blue, indigo, and violet) and use stripes as much as possible. Make simple folded invitations with the word PARTY outlined on the front, and ask your child to color in the letters with different-colored crayons. Invite all the guests to dress in rainbow colors. Make a large rainbow cutout for your front door and hang groups of different-colored balloons from the ceiling or from tree branches in the yard.

Paper baskets
A rainbow of colors makes gifts exciting (page 34).

Games, prizes, and food

Break the ice at the start of the party with a mural (page 49) for the children to fill in with multicolored crayons or stickers. Use multicolored toys and candies for prizes and wrap each prop for the games in a different color. For outdoor games, make rainbow bowling pins (page 48), or provide striped clothes for a Dress-Up Race (page 50). Make pizzas or quiches (page 57) with "striped" toppings and decorate cupcakes with icing rainbows (page 59).

Rainbow stationery
Give out as prizes gummed paper shapes, paints, and crayons in a range of bright colors.

Pom-poms
Make these to add to the decorations (page 30).

Costume
Ribbons on a cloak and a rainbow mask (page 32) make a jazzy outfit.

TEDDY BEARS

Young children will love to have a party at which they and their friends are surrounded by their favorite teddy bears.

Teddy hats
Buy or make a paper cone hat (page 33) for each guest bear.

Cupcake
Make a bear face with glaze and chocolate buttons (page 59).

Teddy-bear cake
This novelty cake (page 64) will be the highlight of the teddy bears' picnic.

Mystery bundles
Include teddy-shaped treats in this game (page 44).

Creating the theme
If young guests bring along their teddy bears, there will be plenty of opportunities for play with the toy "guests." Create the right look with accordion-fold streamers (page 30) in a teddy design and a cutout bear for the front door. Encourage the children to join in the fun with headbands (page 32) decorated with teddy ears or bear patterns. Put your child's teddy bears around the party room and set up a play corner with teddy-bear puzzles and storybooks. If your child has a tape featuring teddy-bear songs, play it as the guests arrive.

Games, prizes, and food
Choose games that you can adapt to the theme, such as Stick the Nose on the Bear (page 41). Buy prizes that are decorated with bears and make "picnic baskets" for the going-home treats (page 34). Make teddy-shaped cookies (page 58), and don't forget the honey!

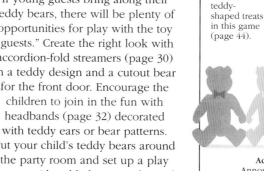

Accordion-fold invitation
Announce the party theme with bear-shaped invitations (page 28).

Bear mask
Stick this plate mask (page 32) on a stick to make it easy to hold.

Teddy bears' picnic
Set out toy plates, cutlery, and tiny sandwiches for the bears to "eat" while the children have their food.

ANIMALS

Parties with this theme can be adapted to suit any age group. Choose animals from the farmyard, jungle, or zoo.

Cutout invitation
Decorate an animal shape with colored paper and crayons for a charming invitation (page 28).

Cutout invitation
Make a different animal for each guest and put them together to make a zoo.

Picture cookie
Decorate a shortbread butterfly with icing and colored candies (page 58).

Picture cookie
This pig is made from chocolate shortbread (page 58).

Creating the theme

Animal characters are some of the most familiar personalities in a young child's world. Buy or make animal party decorations (pages 30–31) and make your own cutouts to decorate walls and doors. As an alternative to a teddy-bear party, ask each child to bring a favorite stuffed toy animal with them. You could draw animal-face buttons for cutting out on dress-up invitations (page 29). For older children, prepare headbands and different animal ears (page 32) and supply crayons; each guest can then color in a set of ears when they arrive at the party.

Games, prizes, and food

In addition to using the animal games on pages 40–41, adapt games by changing the titles or verses. Treats can be animal toys, animal stickers, soaps, or erasers. Call the meal "feeding time" and feed "animal" guests with wiggly cheesy shapes (page 57) or "worms."

Animal mask
Try out these ideas (page 32) for an animal disguise.

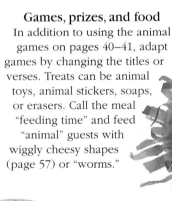

Picture rolls and party drinks
Transform rolls (page 55) into rabbits or dogs and put animal straws in the drinks.

Costumes
Each child wears clothes in colors that suggest their chosen animal.

PIRATES

Pirates are familiar characters from adventure stories and provide a wealth of dramatic motifs for older children's parties.

Headgear
Provide pirate hats and send invitations with cutout eye patches (page 29).

Mobile
Decorate this (page 31) with black ribbon and cutout anchors and cutlasses.

Creating the theme

Dress-up invitations (page 29) are ideal for a pirate party – you could send guests a cutout mustache, eye patch, or even buckles for their shoes. Ask the children to wear a basic outfit of shorts and a striped shirt. Other accessories such as hats and cutlasses can be made or bought. Black, gold, silver, and red are good colors for this theme. Use skull-and-crossbones cutouts around the house; pin one to the front door, stick one on a window, and hang a mobile over the table or in the party room.

Games, prizes, and food

Instead of Pin the Tail on the Donkey (page 41), draw a map of a desert island so that the children can guess the position of the buried treasure. Play Who Has the Key to the Treasure Chest? (page 47), and so on. Make a treasure chest (page 35) as a prize box for goodie bags. Give food a nautical look with small flags, edible garnishes, and icing, and call the drinks "grog."

Swashbuckler
Shorts, a striped T-shirt, and a buckle, cutlass, and hat make a fun costume.

Pirate booty
Small items like these chocolate coins and parrot soap make good prizes.

Hearty fare
Make these edible ships (page 54) for a piratical spread.

Novelty brew
Serve drinks (pages 70–71) with a skull-and-crossbones on each straw.

FAIRY TALES

Traditional themes of knights, dragons, and fairies fire children's imaginations and take on new sparkle at a party.

Toy jewelry
Use bracelets that look like gems as prizes.

Headband
Add a star fit for a princess (page 32).

Party bag
Give this as a going-home treat (page 35).

Knight's helmet
Make this from colored cardboard and crepe paper.

Creating the theme

Choose one particular fairy tale or use a range of ideas and characters from children's legends. If they are given a few props, children love the chance to act out their favorite stories. Send dress-up invitations with, for instance, stars for the guests to make into magical headbands or wands. Reinforce the theme with the decorations, in pink, gold, and silver for princesses, or green and purple to echo a knight's heraldic colors. Hang Christmas lights and swags of white netting on walls to create an enchanted castle, or use streamers (page 30) and mobiles (page 31) to suggest court pennants.

Games, prizes, and food

Wave a wand before an answer is revealed to turn mystery games into magic tricks. Look for Cinderella's slipper in the Treasure Hunt (page 46). Choose prizes such as faux jewels, star stickers, plastic trolls, monsters, mice, and frogs. Serve cheese wands (page 57) and "frog prince punch" (page 70), and make a fairy-tale cottage cake (page 66) as a centerpiece.

Open sandwiches
Cut these in the shape of stars, butterflies, and flowers (page 54).

Courtly potion
Dress up drinks (page 70) with heraldic straws.

Fairy wand
Use a star from a dress-up invitation (page 29) for a fairy wand.

Dragon cake
Defeat the dragon by eating him (page 64).

WITCHES & WIZARDS

Scary things hold a fascination for many young children – a spooky party with its mix of fun and fantasy will send tingles up everyone's spine!

Halloween balloons
Decorate balloons with pumpkin cutouts or cat faces and hang them up.

⚠ **CAUTION!**
Balloons can be a choking hazard.

Magician's hat
Decorate a conical hat (page 33) with silver stars and moons.

Witch's outfit
All you need is a hat (page 33), a broom, and a cobwebby cloak.

Creating the theme

Fall and winter are good times of year for a spooky party. Costumes are easy to create: a ghost needs just a piece of old sheet with holes for eyes, mouth, and arms. For a wizard, make a cloak from a piece of dark fabric with ribbon ties stitched on. Paint silver cobwebs on a black cloak for a witch. For a magic wand, roll up a sheet of dark blue paper, across the diagonal, into a narrow pointy tube. Tape the edges; add star and moon stickers. Make strings of moons and stars (page 31) to hang by the table. To light the table, hollow out a pumpkin and put a flashlight inside.

Games, prizes, and food

Use ghostly sounds like a cat's yowl or a creaking door to play games such as Guess the Sound (page 44). Fill a Feely Bag (page 44) with plastic insects and "witches' hair" (cold spaghetti). Creepy-crawly toys make good prizes. Call drinks "magic potions," and serve with sliced black grapes, moon-shaped pastry bites (page 57), and ice cream with "blood" (red berry) sauce (page 60).

Creepy treats
Buy spider-shaped erasers and pencil sharpeners.

Window mobiles
Cut shapes from thin cardboard and suspend them on thin silver ribbon.

Witches' food
Make a feast with web-patterned cupcakes (page 59) and Red Potion (page 70).

Wizard's hat cake
This decorated sponge cake is easy to make (page 68).

KINGS & QUEENS

Regal characters from children's rhymes, stories, and legends offer a wealth of opportunities for young children to enjoy dress-up play.

Crown headband
Decorate the crown (page 32) with colored foil to suggest precious jewels.

Regal hats
Supply guests with crowns (page 32) and princess hats (page 33).

Creating the theme

Invite children to come to the party as the Queen of Hearts, Old King Cole, the King of the Sea, the Mermaid Princess, or another royal character. To create a regal effect, use rich colors such as red, purple, and gold, together with crown motifs, for cutouts or party mobiles (page 31). "Jewels" can be made from colored foil, then stuck onto crowns or small boxes.

Purple or red lining material makes a silky robe that can be edged with "ermine" made from cotton batting and black paper spots. Prepare gold-colored cardboard shoe buckles for guests to decorate with colored felt or foil when they arrive.

Royal coffer
Decorate a prize box (page 35) and fill with treats like these colored foil stickers.

Games, prizes, and food

Adapt game names and play Follow the King (page 48) and The Queen's Footsteps (page 41). Hand out riches such as "gold" coins or "jeweled" barrettes as prizes. Hold a "banquet" with golden or silver tableware and serve open sandwiches (page 54) and pastry bites (page 57) in crown shapes.

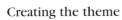

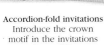

Accordion-fold invitations
Introduce the crown motif in the invitations (page 28).

Royal drinks
Decorate straws with paper coronets.

Fruit kebabs
These kebabs (page 60) look like rich beads.

Picture pizza
Cheese stars and sweet-pepper pieces make the pizza (page 57) look like a royal emblem.

Regal robes
Simple capes can look like flowing robes.

MAKING INVITATIONS

Giving an original party invitation – like the ones below – can be just as much fun as receiving one. Take a little time to enjoy designing and decorating invitations with the help of your child.

ACCORDION-FOLD INVITATIONS

You will need

Paper; scissors; pencil

These folded invitations are easy to make. Your child may recognize the technique from nursery school artwork.

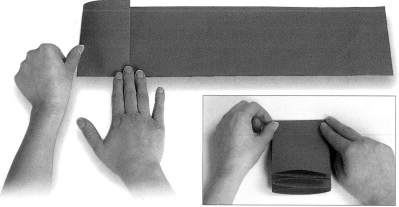

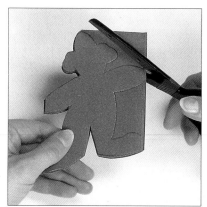

1 Cut out a 20 x 3in (50 x 8cm) paper strip. Make a fold 2⅛in (7cm) from one end, and press it down. Fold the paper back on itself. Repeat until the entire strip is pleated.

2 Draw your design on the top fold of paper, making sure that the design touches the edges of the folded paper at several points. For a clown, leave the hands and feet touching.

3 Cut around the design, preserving the joins along the pleats. Open out the paper. You can write directly on the accordion-fold invitation, or glue one end to a folded card.

CUTOUT INVITATIONS

You will need

Colored paper or cardboard; scissors; pens, glitter, or cotton for decoration

Area left blank for the guest's name and the party details

Cotton tail

Cut out bold shapes of animals or toys from posterboard or colored paper. Decorate each cutout with colored paper and remember to leave space in which to write the invitation.

DRESS-UP INVITATIONS

You will need

Posterboard; scissors; pens; nontoxic glue; glitter

Encourage your guests to dress up by sending them invitations that double up as costume accessories. Draw the outline of the accessory on a piece of posterboard and then write the invitation around it. You could draw a rainbow mask to cut out (page 32), a fairy star, or a pirate eye patch, depending on the party theme.

Star attached to a headband (page 32) for a fairy princess

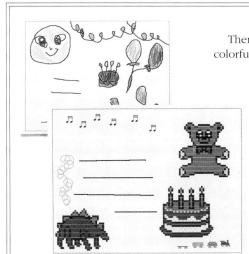

Fairy star
This glitter star could be taped to a short stick to make a magic wand.

Pirate props
Draw an eye patch and a bushy mustache for guests to cut out and wear.

Cutout eye patch is threaded with elastic

INVITATION CARDS

There are several ways to make invitations that look unusual and colorful. Use a computer printout or a color photocopy of the birthday child's own design, or personalize the wording.

High-tech invitations
Using your home computer, print out a design based on your child's drawing and paste it onto heavy paper. The child could also color in a photocopy of his own drawing.

Personalized invitations
Make invitations unique by linking each guest's name to the design; for example, send this card to "Lucy Duck," "Tom Duck," and so on.

Collage of torn tissue paper

MAKING DECORATIONS

Brighten the party room and create a festive atmosphere with paper chains, streamers, and pom-poms. The decorations are easy to make and your child will enjoy helping you.

PAPER CHAIN

You will need

Different-colored paper or crepe paper; ruler; pencil; scissors; nontoxic glue

1 Cut the different-colored papers into 1 x 7in (2.5 x 18cm) strips.
2 Glue together the ends of one strip to form a ring. Loop a strip through the ring and glue.
3 Continue adding new loops until the chain is the desired length.

CREPE STREAMER

You will need

Different-colored crepe paper; scissors; clear tape

1 Cut two strips of equal width from two different packs of crepe paper.
2 Snip along the edges of each strip to make a fringe.
3 Tape the two strips together at one end and twist them all the way along so that they form a spiral. Hang the streamer to keep the spiral intact.

ACCORDION-FOLD STREAMER

You will need

Colored paper strip 20 x 3in (50 x 8cm); ruler; pencil; scissors

1 Pleat the entire strip of paper by folding it every 2⅛in (7cm).
2 Draw a shape on the top pleat, making sure that part of the drawing touches the folds on both sides.
3 Cut around the shape, preserving the folds, and open out the streamer.

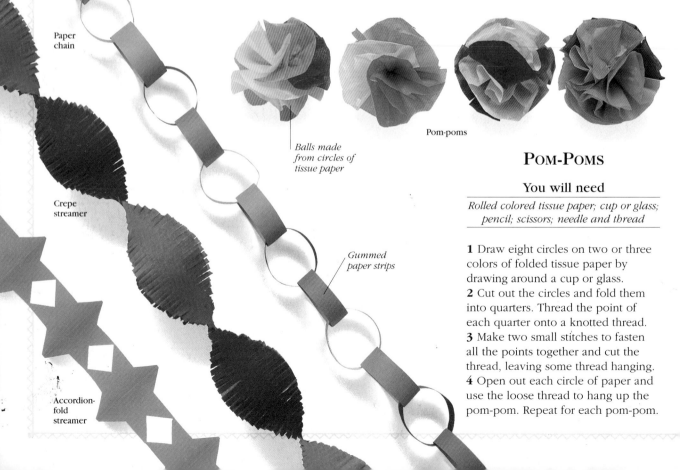

Paper chain

Crepe streamer

Accordion-fold streamer

Balls made from circles of tissue paper

Pom-poms

Gummed paper strips

POM-POMS

You will need

Rolled colored tissue paper; cup or glass; pencil; scissors; needle and thread

1 Draw eight circles on two or three colors of folded tissue paper by drawing around a cup or glass.
2 Cut out the circles and fold them into quarters. Thread the point of each quarter onto a knotted thread.
3 Make two small stitches to fasten all the points together and cut the thread, leaving some thread hanging.
4 Open out each circle of paper and use the loose thread to hang up the pom-pom. Repeat for each pom-pom.

String streamer

Party mobile

STRING STREAMER

You will need

Scissors; ribbon; darning needle; cutout colored cardboard shapes; string

1 Thread the end of a piece of ribbon through the top of each cardboard shape. Knot securely.

2 Cut the string to the desired length of your streamer.

3 Tie the cardboard shapes by their ribbons to the string at evenly spaced intervals along the streamer.

Variation

Substitute streamers or strips of crepe paper for the cardboard shapes.

MOBILE

You will need

Cutout colored cardboard shapes; ribbon; scissors; darning needle; hula or wire hoop; tinsel or crepe paper; string

1 Prepare the shapes as for a string streamer (above).
2 Bind the hoop with tinsel or strips of crepe paper.
3 Cut four 18in (45cm) lengths of string. Tie one end of each length to the hoop. Knot the other ends at the top.
4 Bind the string with tinsel or ribbon. Tie on the shapes.

PARTY BALLOONS

Decorate balloons with gummed paper and put them high up where children cannot reach. Young children can choke on bits of a burst balloon or on a deflated balloon, so always supervise children playing with balloons and clean up any debris immediately.

⚠ CAUTION!
Balloons can be a choking hazard.

MAKING MASKS & HATS

For a costume party or a theme party, use simple materials such as posterboard, ribbons, and crepe paper to create masks and hats that let children act out their favorite stories.

PLATE MASKS

You will need

Paper plates; scissors; colored paper or posterboard; nontoxic glue; felt pens; straws or ice-cream sticks

1 To make faces of animals or fairy-tale characters, decorate each paper plate with the appropriate colored paper shapes.
2 Alternatively, draw a face in the center of each plate with felt pens.
3 Glue a stick to the plate so that the mask can be held up.

Bear mask Lion mask Rabbit mask

CUTOUT MASKS

You will need

Heavy paper or posterboard; scissors; narrow elastic; colored paper or glitter

Rainbow mask

Butterfly mask

1 Cut the paper into a shape.
2 Cut holes for the eyes and elastic.
3 Decorate the mask with paper or glitter, and attach elastic to the sides.

PARTY HEADBAND

You will need

Posterboard; scissors; clear tape; nontoxic glue or double-sided tape

1 Cut a strip of posterboard about 2in (5cm) wide, to fit your child's head. Tape the ends together.
2 Stick on decorative shapes or ears (see animal headband, right).
3 For a crown, cut deep zigzags into a 5in (13cm) wide headband.

Royal crown headband

Animal headband

Streamer hat
To make this snazzy hat, cut a crepe paper strip 12 x 24in (30 x 60cm). Fold the short edge inside a headband (left) and glue it down. Gather the paper at the top and tie it with crepe paper streamers.

MAKING A CONICAL HAT

You will need

String; heavy paper; pencil; scissors; clear tape; narrow elastic (optional)

Conical hats are easy to make and can be used as party hats for guests. Adapt the basic conical hat to make wizard, clown, or princess hats for theme parties (see below). Measure your child's head with a piece of string before making the hat. Use elastic, if needed, to keep the hat on.

1 Use the measuring string to mark out the curved edge of a fan shape on paper. Trace the string's curve with a pencil. Cut out the fan shape.

2 To make a cone, tape down the straight ends on the inside. If desired, make small holes on two sides and thread elastic through.

MAKING A BRIMMED HAT

You will need

Conical hat (above); posterboard; pencil; scissors; clear tape

Adding a simple brim to a conical hat can enhance a costume. You can decorate the brim with stickers or cutout pieces of paper to reflect the theme of the party.

Silver brim enlivens purple hat

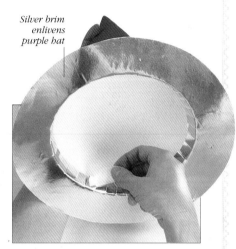

1 Stand the conical hat on a sheet of posterboard; draw around the base. Draw a circle 3in (8cm) farther out and one 1in (2.5cm) farther in. Cut along the inner and outer circles.

2 Snip at short intervals around the inner circle to the depth of the middle circle, making a fringe. Carefully bend up the fringed edge so that it fits inside the conical hat.

3 Tape the fringed edge to the inner hat to make a brim. For a snazzy finish, decorate the brim with paper of a different hue.

HAT VARIATIONS

A hat is the crowning glory of a costume. You can easily adapt conical hats to suit a variety of characters by adding a brim or streamers and decorating with stickers, paints, or colored paper.

Princess hat
Attach colored streamers or strips of crepe paper to the top of a conical hat to make a medieval headdress.

Witch's hat
Make a conical brimmed hat in black. Draw silver cobwebs and stick on gold-paper spiders to achieve a spooky look.

TREATS & PRIZES

Children love to receive treats and prizes at a party.
Choose items that relate to the theme of the party and
make sure that they are distributed equally.

PAPER BASKET

Make a basket for each child. They
can use it to hold any prizes they win,
or you can fill it with treats for them.

You will need

Heavy paper 9in (23cm) square;
scissors; clear tape; posterboard

1 Fold the paper in half four times.
Unfold it to see the paper divided
into 16 squares. Cut once along the
fold of each corner to the first crease.

2 Fold two adjacent sides upward
along the first crease. Tape the
corner square of one side securely
behind the other side, as shown.

3 Fold up the third side and tape
the corner as before. Fold up the
last side and tape both the corners.
Make sure all the corners are secure.

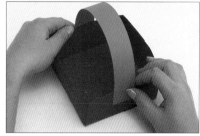

4 Cut out a 10 x 1in (25 x 2.5cm)
strip of posterboard for a handle.
Tape the ends to opposite sides of
the basket. Decorate the basket.

Goodie basket
Make a basket and
fill it with treats for
each child to take
home as a party
souvenir.

Paper baskets

Handle of
contrasting
color

PARTY BAGS

You will need

Heavy paper or strong tissue paper; scissors; colored tape; ribbon

1 For a tall bag, cut out a 15 x 5in (38 x 13cm) paper rectangle. Fold in half and tape the sides together. Tape a short length of ribbon to the top.
2 For a round bag, cut out four 14in (35cm) tissue squares. Put treats in the middle, gather up, and tie with ribbon.

Tall bag   Round bags

PARTY MEDALS

You will need

Large chocolate bars and cupcake liners or round chocolate cookies; gold or silver foil; 28in (70cm) narrow ribbons

These medals are easy to make and ideal prizes for party games. Use small round chocolate cookies or make the medal shapes yourself. Do this by pouring about ¼in (0.5cm) of melted chocolate into each liner and chilling them to set.

1 Wrap the chocolate cookie or chocolate shape in a 5in (13cm) square of foil. Smooth it down. Lay the medal on the center of the ribbon.

2 Bring the ribbon around the medal and tie a firm knot at the top of the medal. Tie another knot where the ribbon ends meet.

*Party medal
The child can either keep it or eat it.*

PRIZE CHEST

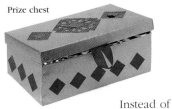

Prize chest

Instead of individual goodie bags, you could make a prize chest. Cover a medium-sized box and lid with colored paper and decorate to reflect the party theme. Attach the lid to the box with colored tape hinges. Line the chest with tissue paper. Fill it with wrapped gifts, such as crayons, candy, or small toys. Each child gets a turn at picking out a prize. Put special items in the chest to match the party theme.

When choosing treats to fill a chest, or goodie baskets or bags, be sure that they suit the children's age group (pages 8–15).

Candy   Springy frog   Toy car   Crayons

Blower

PARTY GAMES

Games are the high point of the party for many children, and there is a huge variety to choose from. Plan a selection of suitable games well in advance.

Songs & Rhymes
Simple singing and action games based on nursery rhymes.

Musical Games
Energetic old favorites requiring only a few basic props.

Brainteasers
Easy guessing or memory games for young children.

Action Games
Team and group games, as well as craft activities.

Outdoor Games
Ball games, races, and outdoor activities.

Entertainers
How to choose and use a
children's entertainer.

PARTY GAMES TIPS

◊ Read through this chapter and choose a variety and number of games suitable for your child's age group (see also pages 8–15). Make a list of your chosen games and props.

◊ Always plan more games than you think you need; it is hard to anticipate how long games will take, as some will be more successful than others.

◊ Avoid competitive games; most young children cannot cope with losing. Plan some games with no winners and others where several or all of the children win little treats.

◊ Write out the order of play. Start with a warm-up game or activity, alternate the quiet and energetic games, and end on a quiet game.

◊ In case bad weather affects an outdoor party, plan a few indoor games to keep in reserve. Some outdoor games can be played indoors, if necessary.

◊ Let the birthday child feel special by starting each game or by choosing the first player.

◊ Adapt the names of games to fit your party theme and choose appropriate props and prizes.

◊ Prepare everything you need in the right order so that the games follow one another smoothly, without a lull.

◊ Adult helpers are vital for games. They can help supervise, operate the tape player, or watch for trouble.

◊ Before starting a game, explain the rules slowly and clearly and make sure every child knows what to do.

◊ Avoid games where only one child at a time plays, or where too many children are "out." Let these children miss a turn, then join in again, or involve them in another activity.

◊ Children have short attention spans, so play each game for 5–10 minutes.

◊ Be flexible. You may need to introduce a quiet game if things are getting rowdy, allow one to run long if it is a wild success, or abandon one that doesn't interest the children.

◊ Prepare to cheat, so that every child has a turn. Be firm but fair with difficult guests.

SONGS & RHYMES

These songs and rhymes are especially good for toddlers and small children, and give shy guests a chance to join in. Go through the songs first, demonstrating the actions, before singing together.

RING AROUND THE ROSY
Action song for age 2 up

(Join hands and walk around in
a circle as you sing this song)
Ring around the rosy,
Pockets full of posies,
Ashes, ashes,
We all fall down.
(Everyone falls down on the floor)

(Sit in a circle with hands joined)
Picking up the posies,
Picking up the posies,
Ashes, ashes,
We all jump up!
(All jump up)

HERE WE GO ROUND THE MULBERRY BUSH
Action song for age 2 up

Chorus
(The children hold hands and skip
around in a circle)
Here we go round the mulberry bush,
The mulberry bush, the mulberry bush,
Here we go round the mulberry bush
Early in the morning.

Verses
(The children copy you as you mime
the actions)
This is the way we wash our hands,
Wash our hands, wash our hands,
This is the way we wash our hands
Early in the morning.

This is the way we brush our hair,
Brush our hair, brush our hair,
This is the way we brush our hair
Early in the morning.

Suggested additional verses
This is the way we brush our teeth ...
This is the way we go to school ...
This is the way we eat our lunch ...
This is the way we go to sleep ...

Ring around the rosy

IF YOU'RE HAPPY AND YOU KNOW IT
Action song for age 2 up

If you're happy and you know it,
Clap your hands.
(Clap, clap)
If you're happy and you know it,
Clap your hands.
(Clap, clap)
If you're happy and
you know it,
Then your face will
really show it,
If you're happy and
you know it,
Clap your hands.
(Clap, clap)

Suggested additional verses
Shake your head ...
Touch your nose ...
Spin around ...
Stamp your feet ...
Do the twist ...

If you're happy
and you know it

GRANDMA'S SPECTACLES
Hand rhyme for age 3 up

These are Grandma's spectacles.
(Make circles around eyes
with fingers)
This is Grandma's hat.
(Put hands over head)
This is the way she folds
her hands
And puts them in her lap.
(Put hands in lap)

These are Grandpa's
spectacles.
(Make circles around eyes)
This is Grandpa's hat.
(Put hands over head)
This is the way he folds
his arms,
(Fold arms)
And has a little nap.
(Pretend to doze off)

LITTLE BUNNY
Hand rhyme for age 3 up

There was a little bunny who lived
in the wood.
He wiggled his ears like a good
bunny should.
(Children put their hands up on each
side of their head and wiggle them)

He hopped like a squirrel,
(Make fingers of one hand hop
up other arm)
He wiggled by a tree,
(Ear-wiggling action)
He hopped by a duck,
(Finger-hopping action)
And he wiggled by me.
(Point finger to chest)

He stared at the squirrel,
(Make circles around eyes
with fingers)
He peeped round the tree,
(Peep through hands)
He stared at the duck,
(Circles around eyes with fingers)
But he winked at me.
(Point finger to chest and wink)

I'M A LITTLE TEAPOT
Action song for age 3 up

I'm a little teapot,
Short and stout.
Here is my handle,
(Put hand on hip)
Here is my spout.
(Bend other arm up)

When I get all steamed up,
Hear me shout!
Tip me over
(Bend to the side)
And pour me out.

I'm a little teapot

39

ANIMAL GAMES

Young children are fascinated by animal characters and will especially relish the opportunity to play the part of an animal in these activities and games.

Sleeping lions

SLEEPING LIONS
Age 2 up

You will need

Small treats for prizes

1 When you call "Sleeping lions," each child drops onto the floor and lies as still as possible with eyes shut.
2 Give prizes to the most motionless children.

FEED THE LION
Age 3 up

You will need

A cardboard box with a lion's face made out of colored cardboard and decorated with crepe paper (the lion's mouth should be a large hole)

A jump rope or piece of string

Balls of newspaper or tissue paper, or soft foam balls

1 Stand the box on a stool or on a low table so that the lion's open mouth faces out.
2 Make a straight line with the jump rope or string on the floor, a few feet away from the lion.
3 Ask each child, "Can you feed the lion?" The children stand behind the line and take turns throwing the balls into the lion's mouth.
4 After a few minutes, see how much "food" is inside the lion. When the lion is "full," stop the game.

─────── Variation ───────
Give older children three balls each, and see who can toss all three into the lion's mouth.

Feed the lion

POOR CAT
Age 3 up

1 The children sit in a circle and choose someone to be the cat.
2 The cat prowls around the inside of the circle on all fours and stops in front of one child at a time.
3 The cat must meow very sadly and try to make the chosen child laugh.
4 If the child stays serious for three meows, he becomes the cat and tries to make the others laugh.

MR. BEAR'S FOOTSTEPS
Age 3 up

1 One child is "Mr. Bear" and stands at one end of the room facing a wall.
2 The other children start at the other end of the room and creep quietly toward Mr. Bear.
3 As soon as he hears a sound, Mr. Bear turns around. If he sees anyone moving, that child has to go back to the beginning.
4 When a child manages to touch Mr. Bear, the two children change places and the game starts again.

──────── Variation ────────

Call the game Grandma's, King's, Kitty Cat's, or Witch's Footsteps.

THE FARMYARD
Age 3 up

1 You need to be a good storyteller for this game. Sit the children in a circle around you.
2 Give each child the name of a farmyard animal – more than one child can be any particular animal.
3 Tell the children to make their animal sounds each time their animal is mentioned.
4 Tell the story of a day at the farm, mentioning each animal several times.
5 Encourage the children to be as noisy as they like and keep the story simple and funny.

Pin the tail on the donkey

PIN THE TAIL ON THE DONKEY
Age 4 up

You will need

A large picture of a donkey taped to a door or wall

A tail made from heavy paper or cardboard and streamers

Double-sided tape or tape loops

A blindfold made from a scarf

A pen or pencil

Bag of small treats

1 Put some tape on the top end of the donkey's tail.
2 Ask the children to line up, and put the blindfold on the first child. Hand her the donkey's tail.
3 Guide her to the picture, turn her around once, and ask her to stick the tail in the right place.
4 Mark the place where the child puts the tail by drawing an X and writing the child's name next to it. Remove the tail and repeat until everyone has had a turn.
5 The winner is the child whose X is in the most accurate position.
6 Ask the winner, or winners, to pick a prize from a "nosebag" of goodies.

──────── Variations ────────

◊ Call the game Stick the Nose on the Teddy Bear, Stick the Tail on the Dinosaur, Stick the Hat on the Witch, and so on, according to the theme.
◊ For a pirates' party, draw an island map; the children stick a paper chest where they think treasure is buried.

MONKEY'S TAIL
Age 4 up

You will need

A ball of yarn

2 identical empty jars

2 crayons

Small treats for prizes

1 Two children play at a time.
2 Tie a long piece of yarn around each child's waist and let the "tail" trail down behind so that it reaches almost to the floor.
3 Tie a crayon onto the end of each tail. Place a large jar on the floor behind each child.
4 Each child has to try to get the crayon into the jar before the other, without using their hands.
5 If there are only a few children, have play-offs between the winners from each pair until you find the Top Monkey and Second Banana.

MUSICAL GAMES

Children love musical games, and they will be glad to dance around to music. To play these games, you will need a tape recorder and tapes of nursery rhymes or children's songs.

PASS THE BUNDLE
Age 2 up

You will need

A present wrapped in many layers of paper (at least as many layers as there are guests)

A small piece of candy or tiny present in each layer of paper

1 Ask the children to sit in a circle. Play music and ask the children to pass the bundle around the circle.
2 Stop the music. The child holding the bundle unwraps just one layer of paper to find a small treat inside.
3 Start the music again and encourage the children to pass the bundle. Watch where you stop the music, to ensure that each child has a turn.
4 The game continues until the bundle has been totally unwrapped. The winner gets the last layer with the surprise present inside.

MUSICAL BUMPS
Age 2 up

You will need

Small treats (optional)

1 Play a music tape of nursery rhymes or familar songs and ask the children to jump up and down, or dance, to the music.
2 Every now and then, stop the music. When it stops, the children sit down as fast as they can. Call out the name of the first child to sit down.
3 Young children will enjoy the game itself. For older children, give a prize to the winner of each round. (Don't give out candy; a child might choke while dancing.)

MATCH THE BALLOON
Age 3 up

You will need

Different-colored buttons made from cardboard and safety pins

Balloons in different colors

1 Ask the children to sit in a circle and give each one a different-colored button. (You can repeat colors as long as there are enough balloons in those colors.)
2 Put the balloons in the middle of the circle of children. There should be the same number of balloons as there are children.
3 While the music plays, the children all walk in a circle around the pile of colored balloons.
4 When the music stops, call out a color. The child with that color button has to find the matching balloon and hold it up. The game continues until each child has a matching balloon.

⚠ **CAUTION!**
Balloons can be a choking hazard.

Pass the bundle

HOT POTATO
Age 3 up

You will need

A big "hot potato," such as a beach ball or some other unbreakable object

1 Ask the children to stand in a circle and give the birthday child the hot potato to hold.
2 Play some music. Ask the birthday child to pass the hot potato.
3 When you stop the music, the child who is holding the hot potato in her hands has to do a simple forfeit, such as hopping on one foot, turning around, or running around the circle.
4 Continue the game until every child has performed a forfeit.

Hot potato

Stop!

STOP!
Age 4 up

You will need

Small treats (optional)

1 To start the game, play some music and ask the children to dance, skip, or hop around the room in time to the music.
2 Every so often, stop the music. As soon as it stops, each child has to "stop" or stand still. Anyone moving must sit down and miss a turn.
3 Start the music again. When the children stop, you can give small prizes to those who are most "stopped." (Don't include candy as prizes; a dancing child could choke.)

—— Variation ——
Call the game Steady Teddies, Posing Pirates, Wooden Witches, Royal Statues, Frozen Fairies, and so on, according to the party theme.

MAKING MUSIC

Young children will particularly enjoy this activity. Saucepan drums and wooden-spoon drumsticks are easy for them to use.

Children love to make noise, so give them some simple instruments made from ordinary household objects. Make rattles and shakers by firmly sealing dried pasta or beans or a few colored buttons in sturdy plastic containers. Put on a tape of music with a strong beat and encourage the children to play along. After each tune, the children can swap instruments.

BRAINTEASERS

Challenge the natural curiosity of nursery and school-age children with these guessing and memory games. Children find the process of deduction both absorbing and exciting.

MYSTERY BUNDLES
Age 3 up

You will need

6 items with distinctive shapes, wrapped in brightly colored paper

Notebook and pencil (optional)

1 Ask the children to sit in a circle and pass the mystery bundles around, one at a time.
2 Let the children decide as a group what is in each bundle, then unwrap it to see if they are right.
3 For older children, write down individual guesses and announce winners at the end.

Mystery bundle shoe

Mystery bundle
toy airplane

Mystery bundle
teddy bear

GUESS THE SOUND
Age 3 up

You will need

A screen of some sort

5 or 6 objects that make a distinctive sound, such as a whistle, rattle, bicycle bell, bag of coins, or tape of animal noises and everyday sounds

1 Hide the objects behind the screen.
2 Sit the children down in front of the screen.
3 Make a sound behind the screen with one object and ask the children in turn if they can guess what it is.
4 Ask each child who guesses correctly to come and help you make the next sound.

FEELY BAG
Age 3 up

You will need

A pillowcase

Balls of newspaper

5 objects with distinctive shapes and textures, such as a spoon, watch, apple, dry pasta, and a toy car

Small treats for prizes

1 Fill the pillowcase with the balls of newspaper and the chosen selection of objects.
2 Hold the pillowcase tightly at the top, leaving an opening just big enough for a child to reach inside.
3 Each child in turn feels the objects and guesses what they are. Make a note of what they say.
4 At the end, tell the children the answers. Give prizes to the winners.

Feely bag

Racetrack game

RACETRACK GAME
Age 4 up

You will need

A ramp made from colored cardboard, or a plank or tray, balanced on a book

A toy car or truck

2 markers, such as crayons or toy figures

1 Two children play at a time. Have a toy car ready at the top of the ramp.
2 Sit the children close to the ramp and ask each of the first two to put a marker where they think the car will stop at the bottom.
3 Let the car roll down the ramp and see whose marker is closest to the spot where the car stops.
4 Repeat with two more children, until each child has had a turn.

GUESS WHAT?
Age 4 up

You will need

Selection of cards, each with the name of an object or animal written on it, such as CAT, BIRD, or CAR

1 One child leaves the room, and the others are shown a word card.
2 Read the word aloud, bring in the child, and ask the other children to mime the meaning of the word.
3 The child has three guesses, then someone else takes a turn at leaving the room. A new word is chosen, then acted out.

—— **Variation** ——
Write simple action words, such as FLY, DANCE, or SING, on the cards.

MEMORY GAME
Age 4 up

You will need

A tray

6 or 7 household objects and toys

1 Show the children the tray with the objects on it for several minutes.
2 Ask them to look carefully and try to remember all the objects.
3 Take the tray away and remove one object, without the children seeing.

4 Show them the tray again. Can they see what's missing?
5 If younger children want to join in the game, ask them to help the older children remember by naming all the objects in turn.

Memory game

ACTION GAMES

These games are just as exciting for the younger children as they are for the older ones. In addition to the physical activities, you can involve the children in simple craft projects.

BALLOON RACE
Age 3 up

You will need

Lengths of string for the start and finish lines

A balloon for each player

1 Lay out start and finish lines on the party-room floor with the string.
2 Divide the children into two teams and give each child a balloon. (All the children on one team could have balloons of the same color.)
3 Each child in turn has to get from the start to the finish line holding the balloon between his or her knees. If they drop the balloons, they have to go back to the start and try again. You may need to join in at first, to show how it is done!
4 When both teams have completed the course, the game is over.

⚠ CAUTION!
Balloons can be a choking hazard.

LITTLE LIMBO
Age 3 up

You will need

3 chairs, 2 with rungs

1 broom

1 Place one chair at one end of the room. Put the two with rungs at the other end, with the chairbacks facing each other. Lay the broom across the top of the chairbacks. Play music.
2 Line up the children by the single chair. Ask them to follow the birthday child as she goes under the broom, then back to the single chair.
3 Lower the broom onto the chair seats and repeat the procession.
4 Lastly, lower the broom onto the chair rungs and ask the children to crawl under it.

TREASURE HUNT
Age 3 up

You will need

Pieces of "treasure," such as large wooden beads, building blocks, candy, chocolate gold coins, or jigsaw pieces

1 Hide the treasure around the house (or room) in places that are not too difficult to find.
2 Ask the children to see how many treats they can find. Watch for children who don't find anything and drop treasure close to where they are, so that everyone finds something.
3 After a few minutes, stop the search and count up the trophies or collect the jigsaw pieces. The children can now eat edible finds or sit down to put the jigsaw together.

Balloon race

WHO HAS THE KEY?
Age 3 up

You will need

A loop of string or rope long enough to form a circle that includes all the children

A key

1 Thread the key onto the string and tie the ends of the string together.
2 The players have to stand or sit in a circle, holding on to the string with both hands. One player holds the key in his or her hand so that it is hidden from view.
3 One child is chosen to stand or sit in the center of the circle with his eyes closed.
4 The others pass the key along the string. When the key is hidden, they shout, "Ready!" and the child in the middle opens his eyes.

He then tries to guess which of the other children is holding the key.
5 If he is right, the children change places; if not, he shuts his eyes and the key is passed around again.
6 Let the child in the circle have three guesses before someone else has a turn.

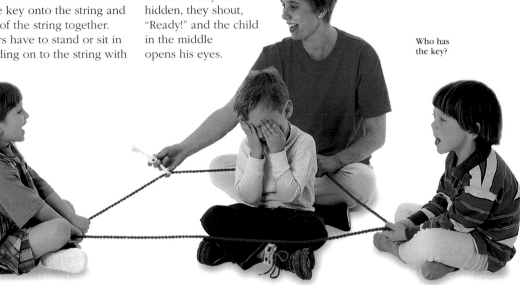

Who has the key?

THINGS TO MAKE

Creative activities are good for breaking the ice at the beginning of a party, and the children will have something special of their own to take home later. Make the activity as easy as possible and prepare all the materials beforehand. Enlist help from other parents.

Royal crown headband

HEADBAND HATS
Age 3 up

You will need

Old newspapers

Headband strips (page 32)

Gummed shapes, stickers, colored paper, colored foil, cotton balls, glitter, markers or large crayons, nontoxic glue

Clear packing tape

1 Spread sheets of newspaper over a low table or on the floor to create a crafts area, and give each child a headband strip.
2 Let the children decorate the headbands with their chosen materials.
3 When they have finished, measure each child's head and tape the headband to fit.

FUNNY FACES
Age 4 up

You will need

Large faces cut out of the illustrations in color magazines

Pairs of blunt-ended children's scissors

Nontoxic glue

1 Give a cutout face and a pair of scissors to each child.
2 Show the children how to cut the faces across into three horizontal strips, so that the eyes, nose, and mouth are on separate strips. Help with the cutting-up if needed.
3 The children can mix and match the sections to make funny faces, or they can glue them onto cardboard to take home.

OUTDOOR GAMES

In good weather, take the children outdoors to play in the yard or in a park. Mark out the play area for these games, staying far away from any harmful plants or obstacles.

Follow the leader

FOLLOW THE LEADER
Age 2 up

You will need

Small obstacles, such as chairs, buckets, large cushions, footstools, or baskets

1 Before the game starts, scatter the obstacles around the play area.
2 The children line up, with an adult at the front. The adult sets off around the yard, jumping over or walking around the obstacles, sitting down, hopping, skipping, waving hands in the air, making funny noises, and so on. All the children follow and copy the leader.
3 After the first round, the birthday child can become the leader.

WIBBLY WOBBLY GAME
Age 3 up

You will need

Pieces of chalk or a length of rope

1 Divide the children into pairs. If there is an odd number of children, ask a parent or an adult helper to join in and partner one child.
2 One partner draws a wavy line on the ground with a piece of chalk, or makes a line with a length of rope.
3 The other child tries to walk along it as if balancing on a tightrope.
4 The partners then swap roles and repeat the game.

BOWLING
Age 3 up

You will need

Plastic bottles

Piece of string or rope

Foam balls or small potatoes

1 Set up the plastic bottles and place a piece of string or rope on the ground a few paces away.
2 Each child stands behind the line and throws a foam ball or a potato at the pins, to see how many he can knock down. The game is over when everyone has had a turn.

Bowling

MURAL
Age 3 up

You will need

A very large piece of plain paper and heavy-duty tape

Crayons

Stickers or pieces of colored gummed paper

1 Tape the paper on a wall and put crayons nearby.
2 The children can draw around each other and color in the outlines, or add gummed paper and stickers to make patterns on the mural.

ROLL A BALL
Age 3 up

You will need

A beach ball

1 The children sit in a circle with legs spread out and feet touching.
2 The birthday child is given the beach ball to start the game. He calls out another child's name and rolls the ball along the floor to her.
3 She then repeats the action. Make sure that every child has a turn.

MAKING BUBBLES
Age 3 up

You will need

Bubble soap and a loop for each child

1 Give the children their own bubble soap and loops and show them how to blow bubbles, gently and slowly.
2 See how many bubbles they can make. Can they make giant ones or catch the bubbles they have made? Whose bubble goes the highest?
3 Have spare bubble soap handy.

Mural

OUTDOOR GAMES

These games are more structured and last longer than the games for younger children. Older children may want to play their favorite game several times, so be prepared!

FREEZE TAG
Age 4 up

1 The birthday child is It first and runs around trying to catch, or "tag," other players.
2 Anyone who is tagged must freeze where they are and stand as still as possible. They cannot move again until another child touches, or unfreezes, them.
3 Whoever is tagged twice becomes the next It.
4 When the child playing It changes, any player who is still frozen can unfreeze. The game starts over again, and each child regains two lives.

DUCK, DUCK, GOOSE
Age 4 up

1 The children all sit in a circle. One child is It and walks around the outside of the circle, gently tapping each child on the head and saying "duck."
2 Finally, It taps a player on the head and says "goose."
3 The "goose" then has to jump up and chase It around the circle, trying to catch him before he can reach and sit down in the empty space left by the goose.
4 If It reaches the space first, the goose becomes the next It. If the goose catches It, the same child plays It again.

PARACHUTE PLAY
Age 4 up

You will need
An old flat sheet, preferably king-size

1 Gather the children around the edges of the sheet, and ask them to hold on to the edges at intervals.
2 Tell the children to raise the "parachute" up into the air. As it billows up, call out the names of two children.
3 The two children have to run under the sheet and swap places before the parachute comes down.
4 Anyone caught in the parachute can join in again.

DRESS-UP RACE
Age 4 up

You will need
Two piles of clothes (each child will need one item of clothing)

1 Divide the children into two teams. Put the piles of clothes next to each other and a few paces away from the children.
2 Each child has to run to his or her team's pile of clothes and put on one item of clothing. He or she then runs back to the team.
3 As each child returns to her team, the next one sets off and runs to the pile of clothes. The first team to use up all their clothes wins.

Dress-up race

ENTERTAINERS

If you are expecting a large number of guests or wish to spend some time talking to other parents, hire an experienced entertainer who can keep the children enthralled.

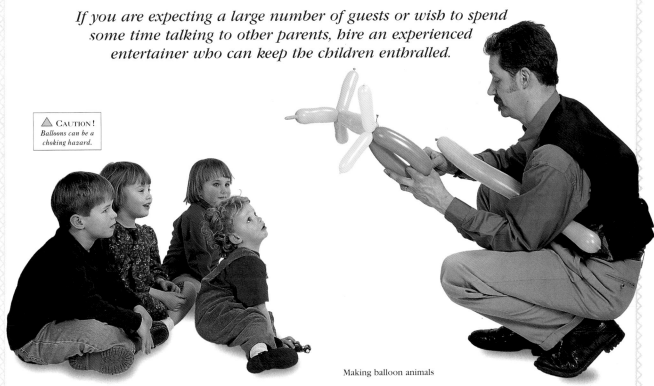

⚠ CAUTION!
Balloons can be a choking hazard.

Making balloon animals

FINDING AN ENTERTAINER

Some entertainers will run the entire party for you, organizing games and overseeing the meal. Others provide a whole range of separate activities, from puppet shows or face painting to conjuring or balloon animals.

Entertainers advertise, but it is best to ask around for a personal recommendation. Find someone who is experienced with the age group of the children at your party. Very young children, for instance, may find a heavily disguised clown frightening rather than funny. Bear in mind the following:

◊ Young children have short attention spans. For three-year-olds, make sure that no part of the entertainment lasts more than

15 minutes. Four- or five-year-olds can concentrate longer, but they prefer a variety of activities.
◊ If the party has mixed age groups, the entertainer should suit the pace of the youngest children.
◊ Ask what the entertainer does for each age group. Does he or she dress up; organize games; provide balloons or prizes?

Once you have chosen your entertainer, book in advance. Then write to confirm the date, time, and place of the party, your child's age, the number of guests, the party theme if any, your address, and the terms of your agreement. A week beforehand, confirm the booking and ask the entertainer how you should arrange the party area.

HOME ENTERTAINMENT

Ask a young friend or relative to put on a magic show by dressing up and performing a few tricks learned from a book. The birthday child could be the magician's assistant.

The show could last about 15 minutes

Party Food

Use a little imagination to tempt small appetites with a feast of savory and sweet goodies that are tasty, colorful, and fun to eat.

Savory Treats
An appetizing selection of finger foods, dips, open sandwiches, rolls, mini quiches, and pizzas, with tips on how to garnish them with pretty patterns or make them look like funny faces, animals, flowers, or toys.

Sweet Treats
A dazzling array of picture cookies, cakes, and other sweet morsels, fruit desserts and ice-cream sundaes in mouthwatering flavors, and homemade summer ice pops with real fruit pieces.

Making Cakes
For the crowning glory of the party meal, use these recipes for versatile, quick cakes and basic icings, then choose from a wealth of original ideas on how to transform plain cakes into magical party cakes.

Drinks
Even children can enjoy their own special cocktails. Here are recipes for exciting fruit-juice punches, creamy milk shakes, and real lemonade.

PARTY FOOD TIPS

◊ Plan the party menu a couple of weeks before the party, to allow time for shopping and preparing the food.

◊ The amount of food depends on the children's age and time of day. Small children each need a couple of savory treats, drinks, and cake. For older children, provide each with four savory treats, two sweet treats, a chilled dessert, drinks, and cake.

◊ Link food to the theme, if you have one. For ideas, see pages 20–27.

◊ Don't forget to provide for parents. Offer them a few savory nibbles and a fruit punch.

◊ Young children are conservative about food, so keep the basic ingredients simple and concentrate on decoration and presentation.

◊ If you are short of time, buy ready-made food and make it special with garnishes and decoration.

◊ Ask your child if he or she has a preference for a particular type of cake. If not, keep the cake hidden so it is a surprise.

◊ Buy a few favorite small nibbles such as plain chips and crackers.

◊ Allow two days for the cake: one day to bake it and the following day to ice and decorate it.

◊ Keep portions small. Little versions of dishes such as pizzas and quiches are fun and easy to eat.

◊ Pour out drinks before the meal; don't leave the pitcher on the table. Have a sponge handy for spills. Ask babies' and toddlers' parents to bring sippy cups and bottles.

◊ Do not leave matches or knives on the table or within children's reach.

◊ Serve "real food" before sweet things; pass around different dishes so that every child has a choice.

◊ Do not worry about how much the children eat. There will always be some who eat nothing but ice cream or chips at a party.

◊ Wrap uneaten goodies, such as cupcakes; add to going-home bags.

SAVORY TREATS

Finger foods are easiest for children to eat at a party. Keep the servings small and be inventive with garnishes – even bread rolls and sandwiches can be made into fun shapes.

Open sandwiches

OPEN SANDWICHES
Makes 16–24 sandwiches

8 slices WHEAT OR WHITE TOAST
4 slices FIRM BREAD, SUCH AS RYE
12 tsp MAYONNAISE OR CREAM CHEESE
About 12 slices each HAM AND CHEESE, OR 24 slices SALAMI

For the garnish

Slices of CUCUMBER, RADISH, OR APPLE; strips of CARROT, PEPPER, OR CHIVES

1 Spread each slice with 1 tsp of mayonnaise or cream cheese.
2 Use cookie cutters to cut out shapes such as stars or animals. Each slice will make 1–2 sandwiches.
3 Cut the slices of ham, cheese, or salami into corresponding shapes. Lay them on top of the bread bases.
4 Make patterns or faces with the garnish ingredients to finish.

SAILBOATS
Makes 12–18 sailboats

1 MEDIUM CUCUMBER
8oz (250g) CREAM CHEESE, OR ANY PICTURE ROLL FILLING (opposite)
3 slices BREAD

1 Cut the cucumber in half lengthwise and slice into 1½in (4cm) pieces.
2 Slice off the bottom of each piece. Hollow out the middle and heap in 1 tsp of the chosen filling.
3 Cut each slice of bread into six small triangles to make the "sails."
4 Push a short length of plastic cocktail straw through each bread sail, then stick one sail into the filling of each boat.

SAVORY DIPS
Makes 16–20 servings

1lb (500g) CREAM CHEESE
6 tbsp PLAIN YOGURT OR SOUR CREAM
SALT AND PEPPER
6 tbsp SMOOTH PEANUT BUTTER

For the finger food

4 BLANCHED CARROTS, ½ CUCUMBER, 1 each RED, YELLOW, AND GREEN PEPPER, 2 CRISP APPLES, 6 BREADSTICKS

1 Mash the cream cheese in a bowl until it is smooth.
2 Mix the yogurt in well. Season to taste.
3 Divide the mixture equally between two bowls. One portion makes a plain dip.
4 Mix the peanut butter into the other portion to make a peanut butter dip.
5 Cut the vegetables into short strips. Cut the apples into slices and the breadsticks into short lengths to make "fingers."

To serve the dips
1 Divide each dip into two bowls, one for each end of the table.
2 Arrange the vegetable fingers, apple slices, and breadsticks around the bowls. Garnish with a few chips.

— Variations —
◊ For cheese dip, replace the peanut butter with ½ cup grated cheese.
◊ For avocado dip, replace the peanut butter with a mashed avocado.
◊ For tomato dip, add 2 tbsp tomato paste to the plain dip instead of the peanut butter.

A thick filling such as cheese will support the plastic straw "mast."

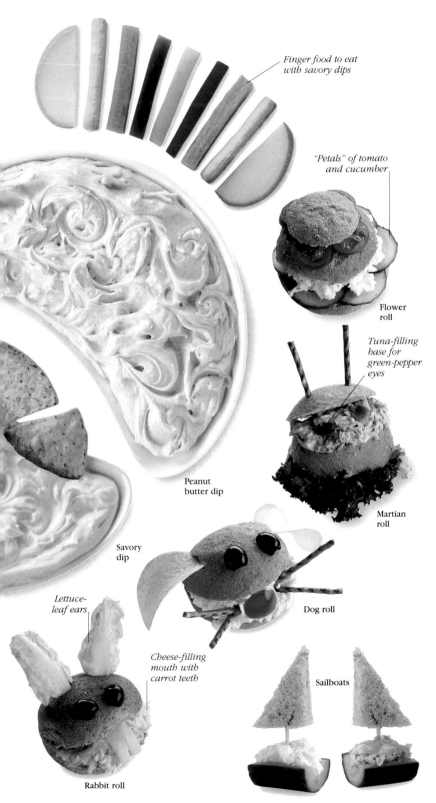

Finger food to eat
with savory dips

"Petals" of tomato
and cucumber

Flower
roll

Tuna-filling
base for
green-pepper
eyes

Peanut
butter dip

Martian
roll

Savory
dip

Dog roll

Lettuce-
leaf ears

Cheese-filling
mouth with
carrot teeth

Sailboats

Rabbit roll

PICTURE ROLLS
Makes 18 rolls

18 WHEAT OR BROWN BREAD ROLLS

For the fillings

4 EGGS
6 tbsp MAYONNAISE
SALT AND PEPPER
8oz (250g) CANNED TUNA, DRAINED
1¼ cup (175g) GRATED CHEESE
1¼ cup (175g) GRATED CARROT

For the garnish

CHERRY TOMATOES, CUCUMBER, GREEN
PEPPER, CARROT, THIN PRETZEL STICKS,
PITTED OLIVES, LETTUCE, CHIPS

1 For egg filling, boil the eggs for
about 10 minutes. Run them under
cold water and let cool.
2 Remove the shells and mash the
eggs in a bowl. Add 2 tbsp of the
mayonnaise, season to taste, and stir.
3 For tuna filling, mix the tuna in a
bowl with 2 tbsp mayonnaise and
add salt and pepper to taste.
4 For carrot and cheese filling, put
the grated cheese and carrot and
2 tbsp mayonnaise in a bowl and mix
together well. Season to taste.

To assemble the rolls
◊ For a flower, slice into the roll
twice, fill the slices, and garnish each
layer with thin slices, or "petals," of
cherry tomato and cucumber.
◊ For a Martian, make two cuts into
the roll. Use layers of frilly lettuce to
fill the "mouth" at the base of the
roll. Fill the top cut and add squares
of green pepper for eyes. Put two
pretzel sticks in the top of the roll to
suggest antennae.
◊ For an animal face, cut through the
roll almost to the other side. Fill, and
decorate with pretzel-stick whiskers,
a halved cherry tomato nose, and
carrot teeth. Make four small slits in
the top of the roll. Slot in two olive
halves for eyes and baby lettuce
leaves or large chips for ears.

SAVORY TREATS

Use small cookie cutters and petits fours cutters to shape these bite-sized treats into tempting and amusing nibbles.

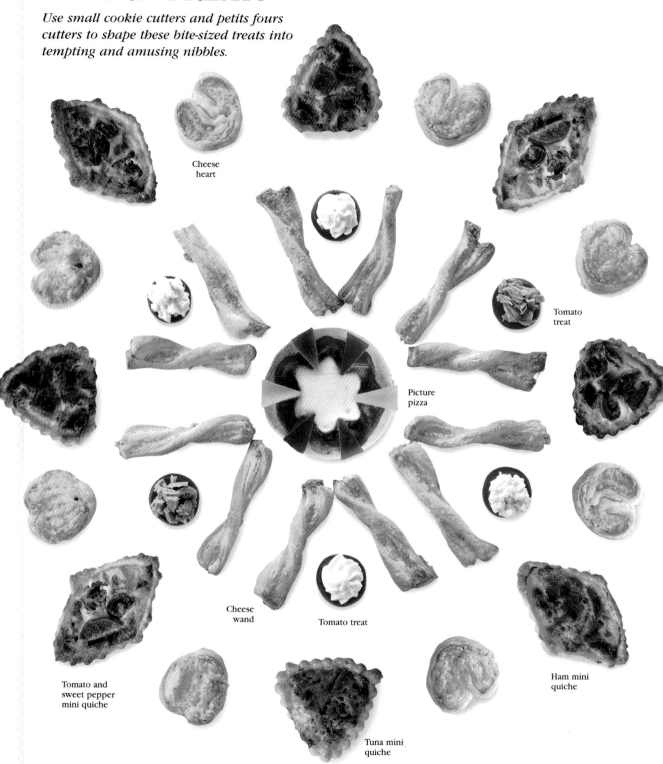

Cheese
heart

Tomato
treat

Picture
pizza

Cheese
wand

Tomato treat

Tomato and
sweet pepper
mini quiche

Tuna mini
quiche

Ham mini
quiche

MINI QUICHES
Makes about 24, using 3in (8cm)
tartlet pans

2 cups (250g) ALL-PURPOSE FLOUR
PINCH OF SALT
4 tbsp (60g) BUTTER
4 tbsp (60g) VEGETABLE SHORTENING
About ⅓ cup (90ml) WATER

For the fillings

GRATED CHEESE, SLICED TOMATOES, CHOPPED SWEET PEPPER OR HAM, TUNA
2 EGGS
1¼ cup (300ml) LIGHT CREAM
SALT AND PEPPER

1 Sift the flour and add the salt. Cut in the butter and shortening.
2 Mix in just enough water to make a soft dough. Wrap the dough in plastic wrap. Chill for 30 minutes.
3 Roll out the dough on a floured surface. Turn the tartlet pans upside down on the pastry and cut around the edges, so that the pastry shapes are slightly larger than the pans.
4 Press the pastry into the greased pans and prick the bases with a fork.
5 Loosely fill the pastry cases with combinations of your chosen fillings.
6 Beat the eggs. Whisk in the cream, and add salt and pepper. Pour a little into each pastry case to fill.
7 Bake for 20 minutes at 400°F (200°C). Let cool.

TOMATO TREATS
Makes 20

20 CHERRY TOMATOES
1 quantity EGG FILLING OR A PICTURE ROLL FILLING (page 55)

1 Slice a little off the tops and bottoms of the tomatoes, so that they sit flat.
2 Scoop out some of the seeds and mix with your chosen filling.
3 Put a teaspoonful of filling into each cherry tomato.

Pizza seal

PICTURE PIZZAS
Makes eight 3in (8cm) pizzas

2 cups (250g) SELF-RISING FLOUR
4 tbsp (60g) BUTTER
½ tsp SALT
½ cup (125ml) MILK
8 tbsp PIZZA SAUCE

For the garnish

SLICED MOZZARELLA CHEESE OR GRATED CHEDDAR CHEESE, SLICED HAM, SAUSAGE SLICES, CHOPPED SWEET PEPPERS, HALVED PITTED OLIVES

1 Sift the flour and mix with the butter and salt in a mixing bowl.
2 Mix in enough milk to make a soft, smooth ball of dough.
3 Roll out the dough in one piece on a floured surface until it is about ¼in (6mm) thick.
4 Cut the dough into 3in (8cm) rounds with a plain cookie cutter. Place the dough bases on a large, greased baking tray.
5 Spread 1 tablespoon of the sauce onto each pizza and cook in the oven at 425°F (220°C) for about 15 minutes.
6 Remove from the oven and make patterns or faces on the tops with the cheese and other garnish ingredients.
7 Grill under a moderate heat until the cheese melts. Let the pizzas cool slightly and serve warm.

Pastry bites

CHEESY SHAPES
Makes 20 wands and 20-24 hearts

6oz (175g) FROZEN PUFF PASTRY, DEFROSTED
1 BEATEN EGG
1¼ cups (175g) GRATED CHEESE

1 Make the wands: roll out half the pastry on a floured surface into a 5 x 8in (13 x 20cm) rectangle.
2 Brush with beaten egg; sprinkle with one-third of the grated cheese.
3 Fold the cheesy pastry in half and roll it into a rectangle again.
4 Cut into strips and twist each strip. Place on a greased baking tray.
5 Make the hearts: roll out the rest of pastry into a 5 x 8in (13 x 20cm) rectangle. Brush with beaten egg.
6 Sprinkle the pastry with one-third of the grated cheese. Fold over each of the two long edges of the pastry rectangle to meet in the center.
7 Brush the pastry again with egg. Sprinkle with the remaining cheese.
8 Fold the long outer edges of the pastry into the center again and press gently together.
9 Cut the roll into ¼in (6mm) slices; lay them on a greased baking tray.
10 Cook all the shapes for 10 minutes at 400°F (200°C) until crisp and golden. Let cool.

PASTRY BITES
Makes 30 pastry bites

3oz (90g) FROZEN SHORTCRUST OR PUFF PASTRY, DEFROSTED
1 BEATEN EGG
SESAME SEEDS

1 Roll out the pastry to a ¼in (6mm) thickness and cut into shapes.
2 Brush the pastry shapes with beaten egg and sprinkle half of them with sesame seeds.
3 Put the shapes on a greased baking tray and bake them at 400°F (200°C) for 5–10 minutes until golden brown. Let the shapes cool.

SWEET TREATS

*Combine cookies and small cakes with fruit dishes and ice cream
to create a truly scrumptious spread. Children especially love
decorated treats that look like animals and flowers.*

Shortbread picture cookie

PICTURE COOKIES
Makes 40 cookies

For shortbread mix

1½ cups (175g) ALL-PURPOSE FLOUR	
¼ cup (60g) SUGAR	
8 tbsp (125g) SOFTENED BUTTER	

For chocolate shortbread mix

1½ cups (160g) ALL-PURPOSE FLOUR	
1 tbsp (15g) COCOA POWDER	
¼ cup (60g) SUGAR	
8 tbsp (125g) SOFTENED BUTTER	

For the decoration

½ recipe GLAZE (right), COLORED CANDIES

1 To make each mix, sift the flour and sugar (and cocoa for the chocolate shortbread) into a bowl.
2 Cream in the butter, and knead each mixture gently into a ball.
3 Roll out each dough mixture and press out the different shapes using cookie cutters.
4 Bake on greased cookie sheets at 350°F (180°C) for 15–20 minutes. When the cookies are cool, decorate with the glaze and candies.

PARTY PRETZELS
Makes 16-20 pretzels

8 tbsp (125g) BUTTER
¼ cup (60g) SUGAR
1 EGG YOLK, BEATEN
1½ cups (175g) ALL-PURPOSE FLOUR
PINCH OF SALT

For the decoration

1 EGG WHITE, BEATEN
SPRINKLES, CHOCOLATE WHIPS, CHOPPED GLACÉ CHERRIES, RAW SUGAR

1 Cream together the butter and sugar, beat in the egg yolk, and stir in the flour and salt.
2 Take a heaped teaspoon of the mixture and roll it in your hand until it is sausage shaped.
3 Shape the piece of dough into a flower, triangle, or traditional pretzel shape (below).
4 Brush each pretzel with egg white and sprinkle on one of the chosen ingredients for decoration.
5 Place the decorated pretzels on greased baking trays and bake them in the oven at 400°F (200°C) for 10–12 minutes.

Chocolate picture cookie

Chocolate-sprinkled pretzel

Sugar-coated pretzel

CUPCAKES

Makes 24 cakes or 48 tiny ones

½ cup (125g) SUGAR
8 tbsp (125g) SOFTENED BUTTER
1 cup (125g) SELF-RISING FLOUR
1 tsp BAKING POWDER
2 LARGE EGGS
2–3 drops VANILLA EXTRACT
PINCH OF SALT

For the decoration

GLAZE (right), COLORED CANDIES, CRYSTALLIZED FRUIT

1 Put all the ingredients in a mixing bowl and beat with a wooden spoon until the mixture is smooth.
2 Spoon the mixture into paper cupcake liners placed in muffin tins or, for tiny cupcakes, into tiny cupcake liners on a baking tray.
3 Bake the cakes in the oven at 375°F (190°C) until they are firm and golden brown. It should take 15–20 minutes for the larger cakes or 10 minutes for the tiny ones.
4 Let the cakes cool. Decorate with glaze and sweet tidbits.

Variations

◊ For chocolate cakes: replace ¼ cup (30g) of flour with the same amount of cocoa powder.
◊ For orange cakes: add the grated zest of an orange and 1 tbsp orange juice to the mixture.
◊ For lemon cakes: add grated zest of a lemon and 1 tbsp lemon juice.

CHOCOLATE CRISPIES

Makes 20 cakes or 40 tiny ones

6oz (175g) SEMISWEET CHOCOLATE
3 tbsp CORN SYRUP
4 tbsp (60g) SOFTENED BUTTER
3 cups (175g) CRISPY RICE CEREAL OR CORN FLAKES
COLORED CANDIES

1 Chop the chocolate into pieces and put in a saucepan. Stir in the syrup and butter over low heat until all the chocolate has melted.
2 Mix in the breakfast cereal until it is well coated. Spoon the mixture into paper cupcake liners, press in the candies, and let set.

GLAZE

Makes icing for 20 cupcakes

1 cup (250g) CONFECTIONERS' SUGAR
About 4 tsp WARM WATER
A few drops FOOD COLORING

1 Sift the confectioners' sugar into a bowl and mix in water, a little at a time, beating well to make a thick, smooth paste. If the mixture becomes too runny, sift in more sugar.
2 To make colored glaze, separate the icing into cups and add a few drops of different-colored food coloring to each. Remember to leave some of the glaze white.
3 Drop a little icing onto a cupcake. Spread it out evenly with the back of a spoon. Pipe different-colored glaze to decorate with faces or patterns.

Chocolate crispie

Iced cupcake

Clown cupcake

Cat cupcake

Butterfly cupcake

Flower cupcake

SWEET TREATS

Brightly colored fruit treats and ice creams reflect the party mood with a pretty display – and they taste delicious!

FRUIT AMBROSIA
Makes 6 portions

1lb (500g) SOFT FRUIT – BANANAS, PITTED CHERRIES, KIWI FRUIT, PEACHES, OR STRAWBERRIES

1 cup (250ml) WHIPPED CREAM

1 cup (250g) PLAIN YOGURT OR LIGHT SOUR CREAM

SUGAR TO TASTE

For the decoration

SLICED FRUIT

1 Use a fork to mash the fruit in a bowl, then slowly fold in the whipped cream and yogurt or sour cream.
2 Stir in sugar if needed, and spoon into small bowls or ramekin dishes.
3 To serve, decorate each portion with different slices of fruit.

SUMMER ICE POPS
Makes 6

1 cup (250ml) FRUIT JUICE OR FRUIT-FLAVORED YOGURT

1¼ cups (280ml) CHOPPED FRESH OR CANNED FRUIT

1 Half-fill plastic ice-pop molds with fruit juice or fruit-flavored yogurt. Freeze for two hours.
2 If using canned fruit, drain and cut the fruit into pieces. Clean and chop up any fresh fruit.
3 Place a little fruit in each ice-pop mold and use the rest of the juice or yogurt to fill the molds. Put in the sticks and freeze again.
4 Remove the ice-pops from their molds by holding them upside down under warm running water and gently easing them out.

Arrange dishes individually or *in a fun pattern.*

Cherry

Peach

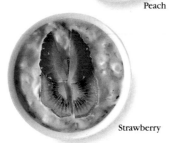
Strawberry

Kiwi fruit

Banana

ICE-CREAM SUNDAES
Makes 8

ICE CREAM, IN A VARIETY OF FLAVORS AND COLORS

For the chocolate sauce

4oz (125g) SEMISWEET CHOCOLATE

½ cup (150ml) HEAVY CREAM

2 tsp SUGAR

½ cup (150ml) WATER

For the red berry sauce

8oz (250g) FROZEN SUMMER FRUITS

2 tbsp HEAVY CREAM

4 tbsp CONFECTIONERS' SUGAR

1 Scoop tiny balls of ice cream and fill eight small bowls with a selection.
2 Pour chocolate or red berry sauce over each bowl of ice cream.

To make the chocolate sauce
1 Break the chocolate into a bowl over a pan of simmering water. Add the cream, sugar, and water. Stir gently until the chocolate melts.
2 Let the sauce simmer for five minutes, whisking all the time.

To make the red berry sauce
1 Allow the fruits to defrost.
2 Mix all the ingredients together in a blender until you have thick sauce.

FRUIT KEBABS
Makes 8

2lb (1kg) COLORFUL FRUIT, SUCH AS STRAWBERRIES, KIWI FRUIT, PEACHES, PINEAPPLE, BLACK AND GREEN SEEDLESS GRAPES, PITTED CHERRIES, AND MANDARIN ORANGES

1 Halve smaller fruits. Peel and slice larger fruit.
2 Thread the pieces of fruit onto short wooden skewers and arrange them on a plate in a fan or circle. Don't use sticks with sharp points.

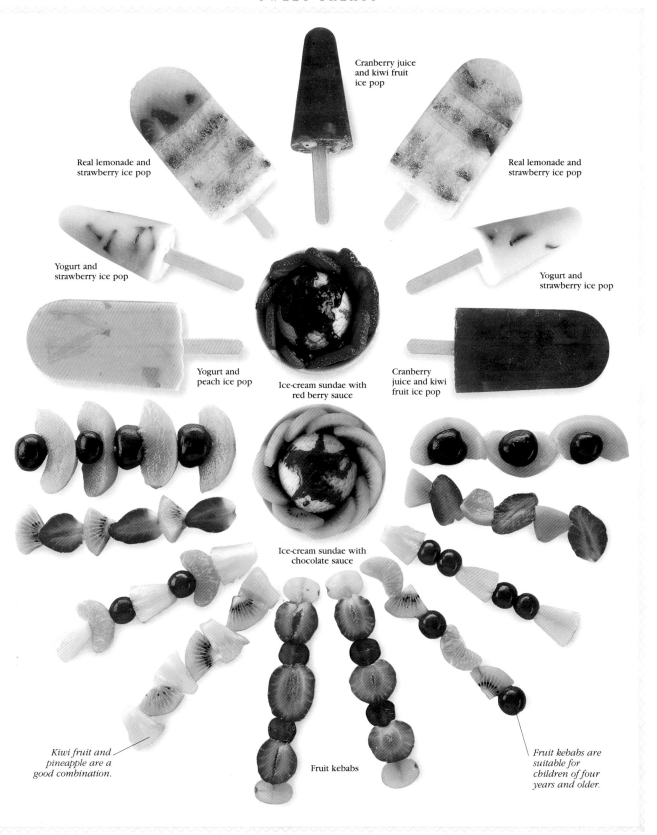

Cranberry juice
and kiwi fruit
ice pop

Real lemonade and
strawberry ice pop

Real lemonade and
strawberry ice pop

Yogurt and
strawberry ice pop

Yogurt and
strawberry ice pop

Yogurt and
peach ice pop

Ice-cream sundae with
red berry sauce

Cranberry
juice and kiwi
fruit ice pop

Ice-cream sundae with
chocolate sauce

*Kiwi fruit and
pineapple are a
good combination.*

Fruit kebabs

*Fruit kebabs are
suitable for
children of four
years and older.*

MAKING CAKES

*With imaginative shaping and decoration, you can transform
a simple sponge cake like the one shown below into a stunning novelty
centerpiece. Try one of the ideas from the following pages.*

QUICK SPONGE CAKE
Makes 20-24 servings

For a 8in (20cm) round cake

1 cup (250g) SOFTENED BUTTER OR MARGARINE
2 cups (250g) SELF-RISING FLOUR, SIFTED
1 cup & 2 tbsp (250g) SUGAR
4 EGGS
1 tsp BAKING POWDER

For a 8in (20cm) square cake

1¼ cups (300g) SOFTENED BUTTER OR MARGARINE
2½ cups (300g) SELF-RISING FLOUR, SIFTED
1¾ cups (300g) SUGAR
5 EGGS
1½ tsp BAKING POWDER

Other options

Use a good-quality cake mix – there are many flavor options available now, and you and your child probably have a favorite. Store-bought buttercream icing is reliable, and the white varieties can be tinted with food color. For a fancy finish, buy ready-to-use fondant and color it.

Variations

◊ For an orange cake, add the juice and grated zest of one orange (for a stronger flavor, you can add a little more zest).
◊ For a lemon cake, add the juice and grated zest of one lemon (for a stronger flavor, you can add more a little more zest).
◊ For a chocolate cake, substitute ¼ cup (30g) of cocoa powder for the same amount of flour.

1 Grease the cake pan. Cut some waxed paper to fit the sides, leaving 1in (2.5cm) extra around the top. Fringe the edge for a round pan; cut into the corners for a square pan.

2 To line the bottom, place the pan on waxed paper and draw around it. Cut out the circle or square, press it down into the base of the pan, and smooth it out.

3 Put all the ingredients in a mixing bowl and beat with a wooden spoon for about two minutes (or one minute with an electric mixer) until the mixture is smooth and creamy.

4 Set the oven to 325°F (160°C). Spoon the mixture into the cake pan, using a broad-bladed knife to spread the mixture out to the edges and to smooth the surface.

5 Place the cake in the center of the preheated oven. Bake until the center of the cake feels firm and springy, for 1–1¼ hours. Let the cake cool for a few minutes, then turn it onto a wire rack. Peel off the waxed paper. Let the cake cool completely before decorating it.

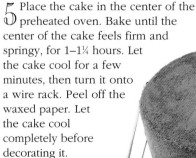

ICING THE CAKE

Give different finishes to cakes by using the appropriate icings. Choose from fluffy buttercream, glossy glaze, or smooth fondant icing.

BUTTERCREAM ICING

This icing is easy to use and to work into a variety of textures, disguising surface imperfections on the cake. It is the best icing to use on a cake for very young children.

For a 8in (20cm) cake

½ cup (125g) BUTTER OR MARGARINE
2 cups (250g) CONFECTIONERS' SUGAR
2 tsp HOT WATER

1 Put the butter or margarine in a mixing bowl and beat with a wooden spoon or electric mixer until soft.
2 Sift and add the sugar, and water. Beat until the icing is pale and creamy.

Variations

◊ For orange or lemon-flavored icing, add finely grated zest of an orange or lemon.
◊ For chocolate icing, add 2 tbsp (15g) cocoa powder and reduce the confectioners' sugar proportionally.
◊ For colored icing, add food coloring, a few drops at a time.

GLAZE

This white icing is easy to make and spreads evenly.

For a 8in (20cm) cake

1–1½ cups (125–175g) CONFECTIONERS' SUGAR
1 tbsp WARM WATER

1 Sift the confectioners' sugar into a bowl and mix in the water, a little at a time, to make a thick, smooth paste. If the mixture becomes too runny, sift in some more sugar.
2 Spoon icing onto the cake; smooth it out with the back of a teaspoon.

FONDANT ICING

Fondant icing gives a very smooth, molded finish to a cake. Ready-to-use fondant icing is the best option; if you make your own, use a free-range egg to minimize the salmonella risk. This recipe makes 1½ lb of icing.

For a 8in (20cm) cake

6 cups (750g) CONFECTIONERS' SUGAR
1 EGG WHITE, PREFERABLY FREE-RANGE
3 tbsp LIGHT CORN SYRUP
A few drops FOOD COLORING

1 Sift the confectioners' sugar into a bowl. Make a hollow in the center.
2 Put the egg white and corn syrup into the hollow. Slowly fold the confectioner's sugar over into the center until the mixture is fairly stiff.
3 Knead the icing until smooth, and add drops of food coloring to the desired hue. Add a little more sugar if the mixture becomes too soft.
4 Roll out the icing on a surface that is lightly dusted with confectioners' sugar. Lift the icing onto the cake and mold it around the sides. Trim.

Balls of colored fondant icing

Candles

There is a huge range of candles now available for birthday cakes. You can choose from classic plain or spiral shapes and "magic" candles that you cannot blow out, or single large candles in the shape of numerals or cartoon figures. Novelty candle holders are great fun, too.

DECORATIONS

In addition to traditional birthday candles, you can decorate your cake with a variety of candies and chocolates to create colorful and realistic pictures.

Licorice whip

Angelica

Chocolates

Milk chocolate buttons

Rainbow sprinkles

Chocolate sprinkles

Candy-covered chocolate

White chocolate chips

Chocolate numbers

Glacé cherries

Assorted candies

ROUND CAKES

Adapt round cakes to make any design that includes curves, such as a face, or that forms a geometric shape derived from a circle, like a star.

Fur effect created with a broad-bladed knife

TEDDY BEAR CAKE

Makes 20-24 servings

8in (20cm) ROUND CAKE (page 62)

4 CUPCAKES (page 59), UN-ICED

1½ recipes CHOCOLATE BUTTERCREAM ICING (page 63)

For decoration

WHITE AND MILK CHOCOLATE BUTTONS, SMALL AMOUNT OF FONDANT ICING, GLACE CHERRY

Make teddy features from fondant icing, chocolate buttons, and a glacé cherry

Use two cupcakes on top of each other for each ear. Cut a small crescent from the side of each so that they sit neatly against the large cake. Paste all the cake sections together with a little icing. Ice and decorate the cake.

DRAGON CAKE

Makes about 20 servings

8in (20cm) ROUND CAKE (page 62)

2 recipes GREEN BUTTERCREAM ICING (page 63)

For decoration

¼ recipe FONDANT ICING (page 62), ORANGE FOOD COLORING, 20 WHITE CHOCOLATE CHIPS, SMALL BLACK CANDY, POSTERBOARD

KEY		
1 Body	**3** Tail	**5** Jaw
2 Legs	**4** Head	**6** Spare

1 Cut the sponge cake in half, then cut out the shapes shown above. Eat or set aside the spare pieces, or use them to add thickness to the head.

2 Assemble the parts of the dragon, as shown above. Using a broad knife, paste the pieces together with icing. Carefully smooth on the rest of the icing, making swirly patterns as you go.

Eye made from fondant icing and a candy

Flames cut from posterboard

White chocolate chips for claws and teeth

Orange fondant icing scales

STAR CAKE
Makes about 30 servings

2 x 8in (20cm) ROUND CAKES (page 62)

2 recipes FONDANT ICING (page 63)

A few drops each YELLOW, ORANGE, AND
RED FOOD COLORING

½ recipe BUTTERCREAM ICING (page 63)

This cake is ideal for a big party
with parents and relatives, as well
as your child's friends. Assemble
and ice it on a large cake board or
plate. You could make the icing in
your child's favorite colors.

CAKE ONE

1 Cut off the edges of the circle to
make a hexagon. For greater
accuracy, draw a template first on
baking parchment, then cut around it.

CAKE TWO

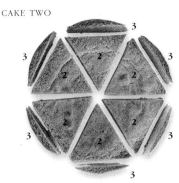

2 Repeat on the second cake. Then
make three cuts across the cake,
between the six corners. Eat or set
aside the spare segments.

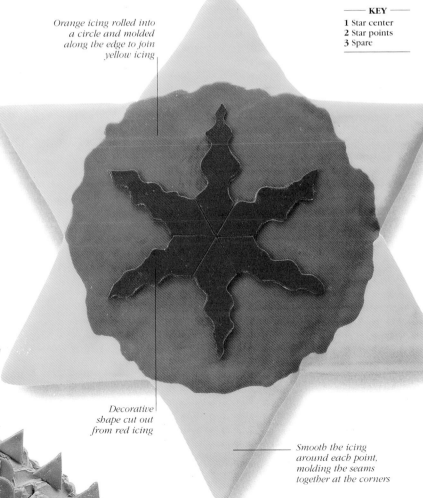

*Orange icing rolled into
a circle and molded
along the edge to join
yellow icing*

*Decorative
shape cut out
from red icing*

*Smooth the icing
around each point,
molding the seams
together at the corners*

— KEY —
1 Star center
2 Star points
3 Spare

3 Place the six points around the
hexagonal center of the star. Use
some of the buttercream icing to
paste the points onto the center.

4 Divide the fondant icing into
half. Divide one half again into
two and one thirds. Color the
largest amount yellow, the
smallest amount red, and the
rest orange with food coloring.
Roll out the icing and cover the
cake with it.

— Variation —
For a birthday cake, cut out an icing
number for the birthday child's age
or the initial letter of his or her name.

SQUARE CAKES

Use basic sponge cakes as building blocks for simple but magical cakes such as the fairy-tale cottage, below, or more elaborate combinations like the train on page 69.

FAIRY-TALE COTTAGE
Makes about 36 servings

8in (20cm) SQUARE CAKE (page 62)
8in (20cm) SQUARE CHOCOLATE CAKE (page 62)
1 recipe BUTTERCREAM ICING (page 63)
1½ recipes CHOCOLATE BUTTERCREAM ICING (page 63)

For the decoration

CHOCOLATE CHIPS, CHOCOLATES, CANDIED ANGELICA, HARD CANDIES, CHOCOLATE MATCHSTICKS, CHOCOLATE NUMBER OR CANDLE

1 Make the two square sponge cakes. Cut the chocolate cake in half. These pieces will form the base of the cottage.

2 Cut the plain cake into four triangles, as shown above. These triangular pieces will form the roof of the cottage.

Chimney and tiles suggested by a chocolate and chocolate chips

— **KEY** —
1 Cottage base
2 Gable roof

Roof ridges made with the flat of a butter knife

3 Stick the two base sections on top of each other with chocolate icing. Ice the roof triangles on their long sides and stand on top of the base in a row. Trim the edges.

4 Ice the entire cake, using the plain icing for the walls and the chocolate icing for the roof. Decorate the cottage with the candies.

Windows and doorframes of chocolate matchsticks

Cottage garden created from angelica foliage and candy flowers

NUMBER FOUR CAKE
Makes about 18 servings

8in (20cm) SQUARE CAKE (page 62)

4 tbsp APRICOT JAM, MELTED AND SIEVED

1 recipe YELLOW FONDANT ICING
(page 63)

For the decoration
COLORED FONDANT ICING SHAPES

— KEY —
1 Upright
2 Crosspiece
3 Base
4 Upright
  add-on
5 Base add-on
6 Spare

1 Divide the sponge cake into thirds by making two parallel cuts. Then cut up the thirds as shown above. Eat or set aside the spare pieces.

2 Assemble the pieces as shown above. Paste the pieces together as you go with the jam. Roll out the fondant icing and mold it around the cake. Decorate with shapes.

Shapes cut out from fondant icing

NUMBER CAKES
A square cake can be cut up in different ways to make a number cake for any age from one to five, as shown below.

— KEY —
1 Upright
2 Base
3 Top
4 Corner

— KEY —
1 Base
2 Middle
3 Top
White areas
are spare

— KEY —
1 Base
2 Middle
3 Top
White areas
are spare

— KEY —
1 Top
2 Middle
3 Base
White areas
are spare

SQUARE CAKES

WIZARD'S HAT CAKE
Makes about 20 servings

8in (20cm) SQUARE CAKE (page 62)
4 tbsp APRICOT JAM, MELTED AND SIEVED
1 recipe FONDANT ICING (page 63)
A few drops PURPLE FOOD COLORING

Moon and star cookie cutters

1 Cut the cake into three triangular shapes, as above. Paste the two smaller pieces on top of the large triangle with jam. Round off the edges with a knife for a domed effect.

2 Keep a small portion of the icing for decoration. Color the rest purple, roll out, and cover the cake with it. Roll out the white icing and cut out star and moon shapes with cookie cutters.

Cargoes of candy fill the cars

Lay down licorice whips for the train tracks.

Small cookies make good carriage wheels.

Train on a track
If you want to make an even longer train, use the spare pieces of cake to make another car. You could also add gingerbread passengers and crew.

TRAIN CAKE

2 x 8in (20cm) SQUARE CHOCOLATE CAKES (page 62)
¼ recipe BUTTERCREAM ICING (page 63)
5 tbsp APRICOT JAM, MELTED AND SIEVED
1lb (450g) RED FONDANT ICING (page 63)
10oz (300g) BROWN FONDANT ICING

For the decoration

¼ recipe PLAIN SHORTBREAD MIXTURE (page 58)
¼ recipe CHOCOLATE SHORTBREAD MIXTURE (page 58)
2 CHOCOLATE RECEPTION STICKS, 1 CHOCOLATE COOKIE, 8 SMALL COOKIES, 2 RED LICORICE WHIPS, 2 GLACE CHERRIES, CANDIES

KEY

1 Cars   **4** Engine front
2 Engine base   **5** Spare
3 Engine cab

CAKE ONE

1 Cut the first cake in half, then cut out the smaller pieces, as shown above. These pieces make the train cars and part of the engine cab.

CAKE TWO

2 Cut the second cake in half, then cut up one half again, as shown above. These pieces will form most of the engine cab.

3 Cut the two squares (1) for the cars in half horizontally. Cut a rectangle out of the center of each top half. Paste the top and bottom layers of each car together with a layer of buttercream icing.

4 Trim the other pieces so that they are level on top. Paste the layers together, as shown above, with jam. Roll out the fondant: cover the cars and engine front with red icing and the rest with brown icing. Decorate.

Spiral Cookies

To make four spiral cookies for the wheels, roll each shortbread dough mix into an 3 x 4in (8 x 10cm) rectangle. Lay the chocolate dough on top of the plain. Press to firm and roll up into a "sausage." Cut into ½in (1cm) slices. Bake as for picture cookies (page 58).

Fondant icing window

Brown fondant icing chimneys

Glacé cherries for headlights

Chocolate cookie boiler

Spiral cookie wheel

Reception stick axle

DRINKS

You can make wonderful drinks just by mixing different fruit juices. Experiment with combinations of flavors, remembering that fruit drinks for very young children should be diluted.

RUBY FRUIT PUNCH
Makes 2 quarts (2 liters)

5 cups (1.2 liters) SODA WATER
4 cups (0.8 liter) RED GRAPE JUICE

For decoration
PURPLE SEEDLESS GRAPES, HALVED

1 Mix the soda water and red grape juice together.
2 Serve chilled, with grapes.

CHOCO-MILK
Makes 2 quarts (2 liters)

3 tbsp CHOCOLATE DRINKING POWDER
2 quarts (2 liters) MILK

For decoration
GRATED CHOCOLATE

1 Mix the chocolate powder into a smooth paste in a little milk. Mix in a blender with the rest of the milk.
2 Sprinkle with grated chocolate.

RED POTION
Makes about 4 quarts (4 liters)

5½ cups (1.3 liters) each APPLE JUICE, CRANBERRY JUICE, AND SODA WATER OR LEMON-LIME SODA

For decoration
APPLE OR CRANBERRY CRUSHED ICE

1 Mix all the juices together.
2 Serve with flavored crushed ice.

Add a decorated straw to make a fun drink

Ruby fruit punch

Choco-milk

Red potion

SUNSET PUNCH
Makes 4 quarts (4 liters)

5½ cups (1.3 liters) each ORANGE JUICE, PINEAPPLE JUICE, AND PEACH NECTAR

For decoration

PINEAPPLE JUICE CRUSHED ICE, PEACH SLICES

1 Mix all the juices together.
2 Serve with crushed ice and a peach slice on the edge of the glass.

Variation

For a sunrise punch, use instead 2 quarts (2 liters) each of orange juice and soda water.

Sunset punch

STRAWBERRY SHAKE
Makes about 2 quarts (2 liters)

5 cups (1.2 liters) MILK
3 cups (375g) STRAWBERRIES
4 tbsp SOFT BROWN SUGAR
4 scoops VANILLA ICE CREAM
1 cup (250g) PLAIN YOGURT

For decoration

WHOLE STRAWBERRIES

1 Put half the amount of each ingredient in a blender and mix for 40 seconds, until thick and frothy.
2 Repeat with the rest of the ingredients.
3 Decorate.

Strawberry shake

REAL LEMONADE
Makes about 2 quarts (2 liters)

6 LARGE LEMONS
⅔ cup (150g) SUGAR
6 cups (1.5 liters) WATER

1 Wash the lemons and finely peel the zest from three of them. Put the zest in a large bowl.
2 Add the juice of all six lemons and the sugar. Boil the water and stir into the lemon mixture.
3 Leave overnight in a cool place, so that the flavor is fully infused.
4 Check that the lemonade is sweet enough and add more sugar if necessary. Strain through a sieve to remove the zest before serving.

⚠ **CAUTION!**
Use plastic glasses for young children.

Real lemonade

First Aid

This section covers the basic first aid needed to deal with the minor mishaps, and occasional crises, that may occur when a number of children play together.

Cuts and Scrapes	Foreign Body in the Eye
Nosebleed	Vomiting
Severe Bleeding	Poisoning
Splinters	Asthma
Stings	Choking

First Aid Tips

It is unlikely that you will have to deal with a serious accident while supervising a children's party, but the antics of a group of exuberant children may result in a child suffering a nosebleed or a scraped knee. If a child has a condition such as asthma, he might become overexcited and suffer an attack. An injured child may panic because of the unfamiliar people and environment, so reassure him while you assess the injury. Put an adult in charge of the group while you tend to the child.

If the child has suffered a very minor injury, such as a scrape, 'treat it and then let him rejoin the party'. Tell the parents what happened when they come to get him. If the condition is more serious, or the child is very upset, call the parents, and if necessary medical help, immediately.

FIRST AID KIT

Keep a first aid box accessible at home. Buy a standard family kit or assemble your own. You could also buy a standard kit and add a few extra articles. Always keep any medicines locked away. A well-stocked first aid kit could include the following:

◊ 1 small roller bandage
◊ 1 large roller bandage
◊ 1 small conforming bandage
◊ 1 large conforming bandage
(conforming bandages mold themselves
to the shape of the body)
◊ 2 eye pads with bandages
◊ scissors
◊ calamine lotion
◊ pack of gauze swabs
◊ 2 triangular bandages
(good for slings)
◊ hypoallergenic tape
◊ 2 sterile pads
◊ adhesive bandages
◊ 1 finger bandage and applicator
◊ tweezers
◊ 1 sterile dressing with bandage

If you don't have the right equipment, adapt a few household items for first aid situations. For instance, use a bag of ice or frozen peas wrapped in a cloth as a cold compress to reduce swelling. If you need to make a sling or cover a burn, a clean pillowcase will serve the purpose.

Some children are allergic to adhesive bandages, so check with the parents before the party. If a child has an allergy, use a nonadhesive dressing with a pad. Keep a variety of adhesive bandages and dressings. Adhesive bandages with cartoon designs are good because they distract the child.

CUTS AND SCRAPES

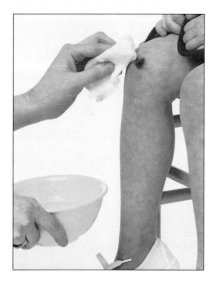 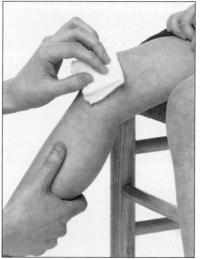 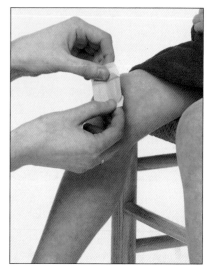

1 Comfort the child and sit her down. Use a gauze swab soaked in warm water or a very soft brush to wash the wound gently. Use a fresh swab for each wipe. Try to remove any loose particles of gravel or dirt. This may cause a little new bleeding.

2 Pat the area dry with clean gauze or a lint-free cloth. Don't use cotton or anything else that might stick to the wound and delay healing. Press firmly with a clean pad to stop the bleeding. If the wound bleeds excessively, see box, below.

3 Dress the cut or scrape with an adhesive bandage that has a pad large enough to cover the wound and the area around it, or use a non-adhesive bandage with a sterile pad. Tell the parents about the mishap when they come to get the child.

NOSEBLEED

Breathing through his mouth will calm him down

1 Sit the child down and help him lean over a bowl with his head tilted forward. Tell him to breathe through his mouth. Gently pinch his nostrils together, just below the bridge of his nose, for ten minutes.

2 Ask the child to spit out any excess fluid in his mouth. If the bleeding goes on after ten minutes, pinch his nose for another ten minutes. Release the pressure. If his nose is still bleeding, repeat the procedure.

IF the nosebleed lasts 30 minutes or more, take the child to the hospital. If the discharge is thin and watery, call 911 or the local EMS. Tell the parents.

3 Once the bleeding stops, clean around the child's mouth and nose with cotton balls dipped in warm water. Don't let him pick at, or blow, his nose, or it may bleed again.

4 Keep the child quiet for half an hour before he rejoins the party and tell his parents about the nosebleed when they arrive.

SEVERE BLEEDING

Press firmly on the wound with a clean pad. Lay the child down; keep the wound raised above her heart for ten minutes. Bandage the pad in place firmly, but not tightly. If blood seeps through, put another pad on top. Call the parents; take the child to the hospital.

SPLINTERS

1 Clean the area around the splinter with soap and warm water.

2 Do not try to remove the splinter with a needle. Sterilize a pair of tweezers by passing them through a flame. Let the tweezers cool. Don't touch the ends or wipe off the soot.

3 Support the injured part. With the tweezers, grasp the splinter as close to the skin as possible. Draw out the splinter at the angle it went in.

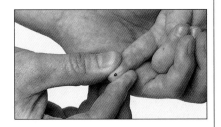

4 Squeeze the wound so it bleeds a little, to flush out any dirt. Wash the area again and pat it dry. Cover the cleaned wound with an adhesive bandage. Let the parents know when they come to get the child.

IF the splinter breaks or will not come out easily, call a doctor and the parents. A doctor will advise whether the child needs a tetanus inoculation.

STINGS

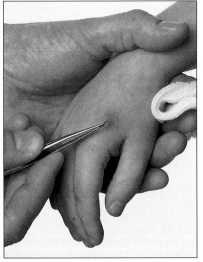

1 If the child is stung by a bee or wasp and the stinger is in the skin, grasp it with tweezers as close to the skin as possible and pull it out. Don't squeeze the top of the stinger – you may force poison into the wound.

2 Cool the area with a cloth wrung out in cold water. Leave the compress in place until the swelling subsides and the pain is relieved. Rest the injured part. Tell the parents when they come to get the child.

IF the child develops breathing difficulties, or collapses, following a sting, she may be having an allergic reaction. Call 911 or the local EMS immediately. Then call her parents.

STING IN THE MOUTH

If a child is stung in the mouth, call her parents and a doctor. Give her cold water to drink or an ice cube to suck. This will keep down any swelling in the mouth that could lead to breathing difficulties. If she does find breathing difficult, call 911 or the local EMS at once.

Watch the child until the parents arrive.

FOREIGN BODY IN THE EYE

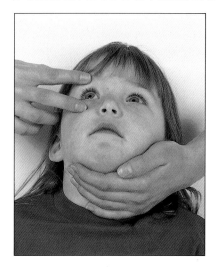 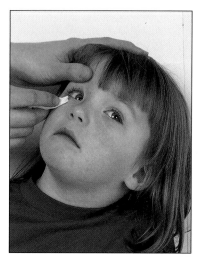 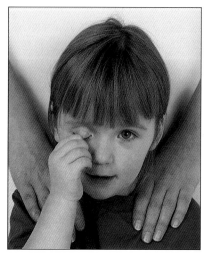

1 Stop the child from rubbing her eye. Sit her down so that she is facing the light and tilt her head back. Gently separate the eyelids. Ask her to look right, left, up, and down so you can examine the eye.

2 If you can see the foreign body, use a damp gauze swab or handkerchief to lift it off. Alternatively, tilt her head and pour clean water toward the inner corner of the eye so that the water washes over the eye.

3 If an object is under the eyelid, ask an older child to clear it by lifting her upper eyelid over the lower one. If the child is too young, do it for her; wrap her in a towel to keep her from pulling at your arms.

VOMITING

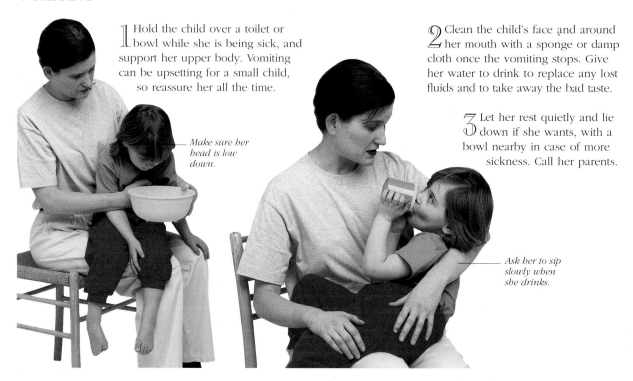

1 Hold the child over a toilet or bowl while she is being sick, and support her upper body. Vomiting can be upsetting for a small child, so reassure her all the time.

Make sure her head is low down.

2 Clean the child's face and around her mouth with a sponge or damp cloth once the vomiting stops. Give her water to drink to replace any lost fluids and to take away the bad taste.

3 Let her rest quietly and lie down if she wants, with a bowl nearby in case of more sickness. Call her parents.

Ask her to sip slowly when she drinks.

POISONING

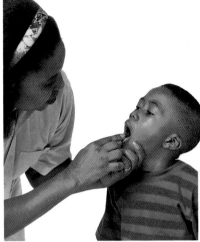

3 If he has swallowed chemicals, wipe away any residue from his face and give him sips of cold water or milk to drink. Keep the containers to show to the doctor.

4 Never try to make the child vomit, as this can cause him more harm. If he does vomit, keep a sample to show to the doctor.

5 If Poison Control advises you to do so, take the child to the hospital or call 911 or the local EMS. Keep the child lying down. Call the parents and stay with the child until help arrives.

1 If you think a child has swallowed anything poisonous, such as drugs, household chemicals, alcohol, or part of a plant, keep calm and try to find out from the child what he has taken, when he took it, and how much.

2 Call your Poison Control Center. If the child has eaten something, look inside his mouth. With a finger, hook out any plant pieces, berries, or pills you can see. Keep any samples or containers to show the doctor.

ASTHMA

Symptoms:
◇ Difficulty in breathing
◇ Blue tinge to face and lips
◇ Anxiety and distress
◇ Coughing
◇ Wheezing when breathing out

If a child has an inhaler, he will probably know how to use it.

Sit her forward with her arms resting on a table.

1 Take the child to a well-ventilated smoke-free room and encourage her to relax. Sit her down at a table or on your lap. Ask the child to lean forward in order to ease her breathing. Talk to the child to reassure her.

2 If the child has special medication or an inhaler, make sure that he uses it immediately. Let the child rest until the attack has eased and tell the parents when they come to get him.

IF this is the child's first attack, call the parents and a doctor. If the attack is severe, call 911 or the local EMS.

CHOKING: CONSCIOUS CHILD

Symptoms: ◊ Clutching at the throat
◊ Unable to speak or breathe
◊ The face may turn a bluish color

1 When a small child begins to choke, encourage her to cough. If this fails to clear the blockage, quickly go on to the next step.

2 Kneel or stand behind her and wrap your arms around her, just above the line of her hips. Make a fist and position the thumb side of the fist just above her navel, against the middle of her abdomen.

3 Hold your fist with your other hand. With a quick, upward thrust, press into the child's abdomen.

4 If the obstruction has not cleared, call 911 or the local EMS. Repeat steps 2–3 until help arrives or the blockage clears. Then call the child's parents.

⚠ CAUTION!
Do not use these techniques on a baby

CHOKING: UNCONSCIOUS CHILD

⚠ CAUTION!
Do not use these techniques on a baby

IF the child becomes unconscious, her throat may relax and she may start breathing on her own. If not, follow the procedure for an unconscious child (below).

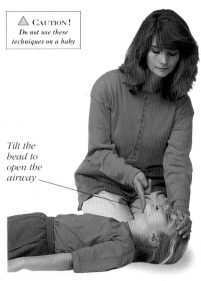

Tilt the head to open the airway

Place one hand on top of the other

1 Lay the child on her back. Check she is not conscious by calling her name and shaking her gently. Open her airway by placing two fingers under her chin and a hand on her forehead and tilting her head back gently.

2 Check her mouth and remove with a finger any object you can *see*. For five seconds, listen and feel for breath on your cheek and look to see if her chest rises before deciding if she is not breathing.

3 Tilt the child's head to reopen the airway. Pinch her nostrils closed and seal your lips around her open mouth. Breathe until you see her chest rise. Remove your lips and let the chest fall. Repeat.

IF the child's chest rises, give abdominal thrusts (step 5). If her chest does not rise, go to step 4.

4 Retilt the child's head and give two more breaths. Call 911 or the local EMS.

5 Kneel across the child's legs. Put the heel of one hand just above the navel. Put the other hand on top. Thrust upward and inward five times. Check the mouth, but do not put a finger down her throat unless you can see an object.

6 If the blockage hasn't cleared but you can get air into her lungs, give 20 breaths a minute until help arrives. If you cannot get air into her lungs, repeat steps 3–5 until help arrives. Call the parents.

PLANNING CHECKLIST

Use this checklist to help you prepare for your child's party well in advance. Tackle the tasks in stages over the preceding weeks to avoid a last-minute rush and unnecessary confusion.

Two months or more before

◊ Visit and choose a party place, if needed. Book the place and confirm the booking in writing.
◊ Hire an entertainer, if needed, and confirm in writing.

Three to four weeks before

◊ Draw up a guest list.
◊ Decide on a party theme, if any.
◊ Buy or make invitations and buy suitably sized envelopes.
◊ Send out invitations.
◊ Arrange for a friend (or friends) to help you with the party.
◊ Ask a friend to prepare a magic show, if needed.

Two weeks before

◊ Write out a party plan.
◊ Plan decorations, menu, games or activities, and treats or prizes.
◊ Make lists of all the items you need to buy or make.
◊ Shop for the decorations or any materials needed to make them, paper table decorations, props for activities or games, toys and novelties for prizes and treats, camera film or videotape.

One week before

◊ Call to confirm bookings of party place and entertainer.
◊ Call parents of any guests who have not replied to the invitations.
◊ Make decorations, masks, hats, party bags, prize chest, or medals.
◊ Buy basic ingredients for any food to be prepared in advance.

Two days before

◊ Check your lists to see that you have everything you need.
◊ Do final food shopping.
◊ Bake the birthday cake.
◊ For an outdoor party, remove any hazards from the yard.
◊ Put activities' materials and games props in boxes in order of play.
◊ Fill party bags, wrap treats, or fill a prize chest; put in a safe place.

One day before

◊ Make any savory or sweet treats. Let them cool, then decorate them if needed. Store pastries in airtight containers. Ice the cake.
◊ Prepare and refrigerate sandwich fillings, dips, and ice pops.
◊ Prepare food for adult guests.

Party day

◊ Pin up the party plan in an obvious place.
◊ Clear and decorate the rooms where the party is to be held, or decorate the party place.
◊ Blow up balloons. Decorate them if required, and hang them up out of reach of the children.
◊ Put out the props for the games and activities, and set out toys and books or outdoor play equipment.
◊ Put the party bags, treats, or going-home presents in a handy place.
◊ Assemble the sandwiches, rolls, or sailboats. Make pizzas or tomato treats, and prepare any fruit desserts or sundaes. Arrange all the food on serving dishes and plates and refrigerate until the party.
◊ Prepare the drinks and refrigerate.
◊ Decorate and set the table.
◊ Lock stair or outdoor gates and block off out-of-bounds areas.
◊ Put tape or film in the camcorder or camera; place somewhere safe.
◊ Dress the family in their party clothes, take a deep breath, and prepare to greet the guests!

INDEX

ACKNOWLEDGMENTS

The author would like to thank
Beata Nagel-Petry for the loan of her books; Carol Watson for her help with research on party games.

Dorling Kindersley would like to thank
Jane Bull for designing and assembling party decorations, invitations, and props; Nick Goodall for photographic assistance; Nicola Hill and Lisa Minsky for editorial assistance; Barbara Owen for supplying costumes, Jessica Bennett and Annette Sullivan for design assistance; and the following for modeling:
CHILDREN: Roshi Bell, Billy and Charlotte Bull, Michael Campbell, James Courtenay Clack, Ashan Craig, Kelia and Keris Cuyun Evans, Austin Enil, Amy Fuller, Anna and Thomas Greene, Lauren Greene, Pippa Hill, James Lynch, Alex and Gina McHarg, Maijá Marsh, Hayley Miles, Chlöe and Freddie Mitchell, Rowan Page, Finn Shannon, Tarahumara Diaz Silva, Natalie Thomas, Ryan Thomas, Amy Beth Walton, and Sam Whiteley;
ADULTS: Stephen Bull and Caroline Greene.

Home economists: Kathy Mann and Jenny Shapter.

Index: Hilary Bird.